1979

DON QUIXOTE:
THE KNIGHT
OF LA MANCHA

DON QUIXOTE:
THE KNIGHT
OF LA MANCHA

MARGARET CHURCH

PURDUE UNIVERSITY
LAFAYETTE, INDIANA

New York: New York University Press
1971

Excerpts from CERVANTES: DON QUIXOTE, translated by
J. M. Cohen, copyright J. M. Cohen 1950, reprinted by permission
of Penguin Books, Ltd.

To My Students
in English 574 at Purdue
University
1961-1971

Preface

This book on Cervantes' *Don Quixote* is the result of ten years of teaching the novel in English 574, a course made up largely of juniors, seniors, and M.A. candidates in English at Purdue University. It is hoped that such a companion will suggest to readers and students various fresh ways of interpreting *Don Quixote* and open avenues to further insights. Some of the material in the book initially originated in class discussions; other material came from the author's lectures. The companion is geared not for the publishing scholar in Spanish literature or for the stylistic expert in the Spanish language but for the general reader and student of *Don Quixote* in translation. It is hoped that this book will enlarge the horizons of such readers and serve as a helpful guide in conjunction with the study of the novel itself. The intention has been to select from each of the chapters only certain points which have seemed to the author of particular thematic interest. No attempt to cover all themes in the novel has been made. However, the main thread that runs through *Don Quixote,* discovery of self in a world permeated by the ambiguity of truth and illusion, real and ideal, will be seen to be the unifying principle behind the companion. The aim of the book is to enable the student to become aware of some of the many compelling ways in which Cervantes' genius manifested itself. I owe a debt of gratitude to all students in English 574 with whom I have shared the reading of *Don Quixote*.*

I am also indebted to Professor William T. Stafford of the Department of English at Purdue University, at whose suggestion I submitted this manuscript to the New York University Press. Mr. Miguel Palacio, a graduate student in my course in the continental novel, has given me invaluable assistance in translating the books by Martín de Riquer and J. A. Maravall. For her accurate typing and retyping of the manuscript, I am grateful to Mrs. E. E. Kildahl of West Lafayette.

Finally, without the suggestions of Professor Anthony N. Zahareas, Chairman of the Spanish Department at New York University, and Professor Gerald Gillespie, Professor of Comparative Literature at SUNY at Binghamton, the entire project would have remained incomplete. Their extensive knowledge of *Don Quixote* and of the criticism which surrounds it has enabled them to give me both sensitive and perceptive advice in the final stages of the writing of this book.

Margaret Church
Lafayette, Indiana

---

* Page numbers in the text, unless preceded by letters, refer to the Penguin Classics translation (1950) done by J. M. Cohen. It is suggested that the explication be read in conjunction with the text.

Contents

Don Quixote, 1615   71

Introduction

That *Don Quixote,* one of the most loved and widely read books ever written, should need to be "explained" suggests the paradox of all criticism. The critic interprets a book that has already been interpreted and understood by many, and yet, if the book has any worth at all, it will have been only partially understood or "misunderstood" in parts by any particular reader. The critic himself adds his own understandings and "misunderstandings," for who is to say from what perspective a true judgment may be made (the lesson, incidentally, of *Don Quixote* itself). Criticism (and teaching) of literature at its best, then, only suggests further ways of looking at a work, ways that may add to the reader's understanding and in some instances may contradict it. Either end is a useful end, the critic as foil, as abrasive, or the critic as an abettor of the reader's own insights. For the essential function of the critic is *re-creation,* building upon a past work which he thereby helps to *preserve,* thus adding to or modifying the insights of the past.

It is with these premises in mind that I make the following critical comments. I have found in *Don Quixote* an everlasting source of delight and new meaning, and my study can only begin to look into the depths of this classic which changes shape under one's very gaze. I hope, then, that what I say in these pages will not serve to dull the perception of others with a plethora of pedantic detail but will transmit the enthusiasm of one reader for a book which is without doubt a document of "the best that has been thought and said" by our Western culture.

I.

Before examining *Don Quixote* in more specific ways, it will be well to indicate some of its thematic and structural connections with European fiction in which it plays a central and germinal role. Most Spanish criticism, epitomized by that of the great critic, Miguel de Unamuno, has idealized Don Quixote as a romantic hero. Another equally important critic, José Ortega y Gasset, however, recognizes the full import of the satire in *Don Quixote* and stresses the book's aesthetic and metaphysical significances. When we examine Cervantes' dialectic, we must recognize that the element of romantic idealization is surely present in the novel, but at the same time satiric and philosophical aspects must not be ignored. Neither emphasis by itself does full justice to the richness and complexity of this work. An examination of the position of the novel in the mainstream of European fiction will serve to prove the point.

The theme of the reformation of man, of society, and of the state was, as José Antonio Maravell shows, one inherited by Cervantes from both the Middle Ages and the Renaissance (which Maravall interprets as a single continuing and integrated period [MAR, 16].* The subject of chivalry in *Don Quixote* cannot, therefore, be fully understood without recognizing both its idealistic aspects as suggested in the medieval practice of arms, whereby virtue and nobility of spirit might be acquired, and its sometimes more superficial aspects as delineated by the chivalric romance. The theme of reform, therefore, appears both in the implicit criticism of Cervantes' satire and in the utopia envisioned by Don Quixote in his dreams. *Don Quixote* must first be viewed, then, as containing ambiguous and antithetical elements from the tra-

---

* The bibliography at the end of this volume should be consulted for sources and for symbols used for sources.

dition of arms and from the chivalric romance and as a descendant of both.

Don Quixote, as David Grossvogel points out, is also the
descendant of still another tradition, "the picaresque genre"
(GRO, 106). A tale of a journey told as a parody of literature,
the novel is developed through the relation between its structure
and the character of Don Quixote. In comparison with its picaresque predecessors, *Don Quixote* both broadens the base of action
by introducing the theme of perspectivism and broadens the
concept of character by molding its hero as both paradigm and
fool, the last fool to cause the world to see the wisdom of its folly
(K, 296). Picaresque elements, then, are remolded to merge with
elements of a new genre. Don Quixote is not a picaro, nor is Cervantes' novel picaresque in any definitive sense.

Cervantes' novel also relates to the pastoral tradition. Earlier,
he had written his own pastoral novel, *La Galatea.* But the pastoral elements in *Don Quixote* are merely interludes and contrast
sharply with the main action of the novel. How seriously Cervantes viewed the pastoral tradition in 1605 must be questioned.
In his story of the goatherd Lope Ruiz attempting to escape from
the shepherdess Torralba, Sancho unintentionally ridicules all
pastoral romances. And when, near the end of the 1615 book,
Don Quixote suggests to Sancho that they turn shepherds, naming
themselves Quixotiz and Panzino and mourning absent beauty in
rustic solitude, it is clear that pastoral matters, like so many other
matters, are the objects of Cervantes' parody. In the 1605 book
the pastoral scenes (whether with intent or not) are inserted between the more pivotal scenes, which serves both to underline
the wooden character of shepherd and shepherdess and to develop
the dynamic central figure of Don Quixote.

Thus an important way in which *Don Quixote* contributes
to the tradition of fiction is through structure. Herman Meyer
shows how Cervantes' use of the quotation creates a unity through
a harmony of contrasts which Rabelais had been able merely to
approximate (ME, 71). Later Sterne, using quotation in a different way, deliberately creates a sense of discontinuity, in an
attempt to imitate the reality of life. Cervantes regulates structure
through the inner contradictions of his characters. Fielding and

Sterne, on the contrary, are more concerned with outer form [PF, 13]. Sterne, as he himself admits, inserts "a good quantity of heterogeneous matter" [ME, 93] in order to balance wisdom and folly as they are balanced in life, a statement suggesting stress on both the outer form of literature and the outer form of society. Cervantes, on the contrary, would have us view the shadows on the wall of Plato's cave as though they were realities.

Cervantes' awareness of an inner level of reality must lead us to consider his consciousness of inner and outer time, which places him as a major forerunner of the modern novelist. Cervantes' technical virtuosity in expressing this awareness, however, is baroque; poets such as Marino, Crashaw, and Góngora developed new techniques for conveying "a notion of time viewed through eternity" (NEL, 162), time as both "contingent and manipulatable" (NEL, 161). In Cervantes, a sense of inner time —as opposed to exterior considerations of day, hour, or minute— is strengthened by the mechanical nature of his chapter divisions. As Raymond Willis shows (WP), these do not coincide with the flow of the narrative, but, as clock time foils the sense of inner flow in real life, they foil the sense of flow in the novel, evidence of Cervantes' mimetic genius. For the mechanically dictated chapter divisions only serve to stress the existence of another, more valid time sequence in which events overlap and coincide as they do within the human mind.

The present of *Don Quixote* is Cervantes' (or Cide's) recent past, "not long ago," as we learn in Chapter 1—that is, within Cervantes' memory. The past of the chivalric romance is, however, a distant and ideal past, only read about, not experienced by Cervantes or his hero. As with a baroque poem like "Lycidas," the structure of the novel is evolved through "identifying or reconciling time planes" (NEL, 79), through the coexistence, as Thomas Mann would say, of "once upon a time" and "always." Therefore, Don Quixote is both knight and hidalgo. Re-enacting the role of knight, Don Quixote is viewed in the 1605 novel as a foolish and misguided imitator of chivalric forms. Gradually, however, as the 1615 book progresses, we see Don Quixote beginning to assume the inner virtues of humility, understanding, and self-knowledge implied in the chivalric code he is so fond of reciting. In this way a temporal paradox is established whereby past and present become one in the eternity of chivalric values. The fluctuation of withdrawal and participation patterns, which forms the structure of the 1605 novel, and the tension between image and the image as seen in the mirror, the basis of the structure in the 1615 novel, parallel and make manifest the temporal paradox of simultaneous withdrawal into a chivalric past and participation in the real world of the present. An understanding, then, of the inner nature of time allows Cervantes to set up a structure based on the "contradictory reconciliation of time planes" (NEL, 79). Don Quixote's final recognition of the meaning of "true" knighthood is thus shown to be "a conquering of time through time" (NEL, 80), an awareness that "real" knighthood may be re-enacted in any age and that knights are citizens of La Mancha as well as citizens of the world.

It is this particular achievement of the Baroque age that Cervantes hands down to the modern novelist where it is to be seen in his contradictory reconciliation of past and present, of time and time again; in his consciousness of role and of the fact that Finnegans awake; in his "point counterpoint"; in his use of fable, myth, and legend; in the levels of his symbolism; and in the river of Henri Bergson's *la durée*.

We must not overlook other significant links between *Don Quixote* and literary tradition, for example the *theatrum mundi* theme, (see discussion of Chapter 12, *Don Quixote*, 1615), which Cervantes inherits from ancient Greece (Plato) and from the Middle Ages (*Policraticus* and other sources) and which Calderón, Shakespeare, and others employed in Renaissance drama. Nor should one fail to mention Cervantes' use of medieval etymology which proposed many sources and various meanings for any given word. As a "falso cronicón," the inheritor of the fifteenth-century practice of deliberate falsification by historians, Cervantes, as Bruce Wardropper proves (WARD, 10), produces the tension between reality and illusion in his novel. And in creating Sancho and Don Quixote, Cervantes, in the tradition of the *Poema del Cid, La Celestina,* and *Lazarillo de Tormes,* provides for literature and for the modern novel, heroes who encompass both the destiny of man and yet his ordinary, everyday existence (WS, 210).

The position, then, of *Don Quixote* in the light of and as a part of all these traditions is an ambiguous one. Both Ortega y Gasset and Unamuno are right: Chivalric knights of old, picaros with "hearts of gold," a sense of man's inner life, of the value of illusion, and of the universal human predicament, are all present in *Don Quixote*. At the same time we see, as Ortega points out, that Don Quixote is mad and foolish, a parody of knights of old, that hearts of picaros are not always "hearts of gold," that over and above the spiritual significances of the book rests Ortega's judgment of reality as the "leaven of the myth" (ORT, 138).

II.

Friedrich Schlegel stated in 1799 that Cervantes was "one of the most purposeful of artists" as far as "artfully ordered confusion," "symmetry of antitheses," and "alternation of enthusiasm and irony" were concerned (IM, 121). The "architectonic symmetry of parallels and contrasts" is, as Raymond Immerwahr shows, far more carefully worked out in *Don Quixote* than in the usual picaresque tale. In investigating the structure of *Don Quixote* such critics as J. Casalduero,* Knud Togeby,* Raymond Immerwahr,* and A. A. Parker * are notable. In this introduction I will suggest a psychological basis for the structure (somewhat different from the psychological basis A. A. Parker (PF) suggests and yet complementary). The structure which is proposed here includes both the main actions and the digressions and is based on the themes of the book as they appear in my explication of the text. Unless some kind of overall structure is kept in mind, the pages of commentary on individual chapters may appear to be without focus.

The central issue which confronts Don Quixote in the 1605 novel is his relation to other people and to his society. In contrast, the 1615 novel, which is full of reflexive imagery, mainly concern's Don Quixote's discovery of himself. The 1605 *Quixote* was

---

* The bibliography at the end of this volume should be consulted for sources and for symbols used for sources.

originally published in four parts (Part I: Chapters 1-8; Part II: Chapters 9-14; Part III: Chapters 15-27; Part IV: Chapters 28-52). Parts I and II are a unit that describes the first mistaken involvements of Don Quixote in the lives of others and his consequent withdrawal into pastoral solitude. Part III concerns the second sally of Don Quixote and his second retirement, this time to the Sierra Morena; Part IV deals with Don Quixote's role at the inn, with the love affairs of several young couples, with readings and conversations, and with his final retreat in a cage to his home.

In connection with Cervantes' divisions of *Don Quixote* into chapters and parts, it is important to keep in mind Raymond Willis's *The Phantom Chapters of the "Quijote."* He interprets the closures in the novel as mechanical devices which contrast with the durational flow of the subject matter. Willis shows how Cervantes continually violated a sense of the chapter as a discrete unit in the interests of a transcendent unity achieved by means of stylistic liaison. This theory does not, of course, deny the validity of a structural analysis, particularly one based on the hero's psychological development. The lack of logic in the divisions produces a natural flow in the novel, creating and recreating character.

Furthermore, Cervantes introduces four main digressions (or episodic narratives) at key points in the structure to parallel the particular psychological state of Don Quixote at each point as I shall explain in some detail in following paragraphs. Thus the Marcela episode concludes Part II; Cardenio's tale concludes Part III; "The Tale of Foolish Curiosity" stands near the beginning of Part IV, which concludes with the narrative of Anselmo and Eugenio, both deserted by their beloved and withdrawn into pastoral existence.

A closer examination of the psychological pattern outlined above, a pattern of involvement and of retreat, in the 1605 novel, will indicate the basic nature of the odyssey Don Quixote takes in this book, for Cervantes' genius as a writer lies in his treatment and understanding of the inner man behind the mask which he may wear.

The melancholy state of Quixada is readily apparent in Chapter 1; for most of the year he has given himself up to the reading of books of chivalry, so much so that he has forgotten his estate and even his hunting. This fantasy world of Quixada sets the stage for the acting out of his fantasies, when as Don Quixote, he sets forth into the world. However, soon after he is knighted, he receives the first thrashing of many which are to follow. To the laborer who rescues Don Quixote after his beating by the mule-teer, the Don asserts undaunted that he may be the twelve peers of France and the nine worthies all together. The return to the village at the end of this episode does not, therefore, constitute a psychological return or defeat. Don Quixote, despite his beating, is inwardly unchanged and simply reinforces his original posi-tion by joining up with Sancho and taking along some clean shirts and a purse of money. The conclusion of Part I is more a mechani-cal division than a thematic ending; Cervantes creates a feeling of suspense by means of the unfinished fight with the Basque. Parts I and II, as has been noted, are thematically continuous and conclude with the self-imposed exile of Marcela which coincides with Don Quixote's own withdrawal among the goatherds whom he eulogizes in his "noble savage" speech.

The subplots, or episodes concerning characters other than Don Quixote, are always comparable with or in contrast to the main plot (the same parallelism of plots seen, for example, in Shakespeare's plays). Thus the inquisition of the books, in which the barber and the curate employ themselves on Don Quixote's return, parallels in essence the pursuits and methods of the hero himself, for the inquisition scene brings up the question of how one goes about establishing a set of ideals; how, in other words, man promotes his idealism within his society. And the curate and the barber mistakenly use the same method employed by Don Quixote himself. They take up "arms"; they use physical means, the bon-fire, to deal with something intangible, to purge their friend of his fantasies. This is what is meant by mistaken involvement with reality. The essential difference in the attack made by the curate and barber on the books and those made by Don Quixote on the exterior world is that the aims of the former are negative, that is, they would destroy without substituting a transcendent reality. However, Don Quixote himself, although employing mistaken means, is motivated by a positive idealism, by a desire to establish the chivalric mode. As foils, then, the curate and the barber perform a valuable function in enabling us to observe the complexities of human interrelationships and placing in relief the relative sanity of the madman compared with the insanity of those who claim to be sane.

The symbol of the windmill is perhaps a most significant one, coming as it does near the conclusion of Part I. The windmill channels a natural force, and it may symbolize, at an early point in the narrative, the very control Don Quixote lacks in his inability to direct his own powers. It is this symbol of control which Don Quixote attacks.

And although in the succeeding episode the Basque is overcome by Don Quixote, he is engaged in righting a wrong (a capricious blocking of the highway), the very role Don Quixote envisages for himself. Furthermore, the empty ritual, the demand that the Basque present himself to Dulcinea, is, of course, never carried out. It is actually Don Quixote who suffers the defeat, although he does not recognize it as one.

It is after this particular series of misadventures, culminating with the adventure with the Basque, that Don Quixote makes his first withdrawal into a pastoral setting among the goatherds. Here he delivers a long eulogy on the golden age of the ancients when innocence and simplicity reigned, a eulogy wherein he retreats into the past.

His withdrawal is paralleled by the story told to him by the goatherds, the story of Marcela, who like Don Quixote eschews reality for a fantasy world of freedom in the solitude of nature. Marcela's defense of her position is full of the same blatant rationalizations employed by Don Quixote in the defense of his chivalric role. Both feel they were "born free"; neither recognizes the unrelenting nature of the social contract nor a constructive and realistic means for carrying out their idealisms within the social frame. (It is not the intention of all men, as Marcela seems to think, to rob women of their beauty for selfish pleasure.) And yet, like the barber and the curate with their inquisition of books, Marcela also acts as a foil for Don Quixote. Her retirement is self-imposed and springs from fear and negation of the outside world; Don Quixote's retirement among the goatherds contains a posi-

tive note of peace, a return to nature in order to gather strength
for the next sally into combat with the world of material values.

The end of Part II in the 1605 novel marks, then, the first
definite division in terms of the psychological development of the
hero. A sally, born of a crazed fantasy life, has been made and has
ended in pastoral retirement. A new beginning, an issuing forth
into the midst of the Yanguesans, on a nag drawn to some mares,
provides a sharp contrast to the episode concerning the prudish
Marcela as does the bedroom sequence in the inn which follows.
The episodes which make up Part III all illustrate the increasingly
mistaken involvements of the hero, which lead to a fear of the
Holy Brotherhood and of constituted social authority and to a
second retirement, one more crazed and less purposeful than
the first.

Part III starts with Don Quixote's first really destructive act,
the slaying of seven sheep. More serious is the broken leg of the
Master of Arts in the adventure with the corpse. The title of the
chapter containing the episode of the fulling mills reads: "Of the
unparalleled Adventure achieved by the valorous Don Quixote de
la Mancha with less peril than any ever achieved by any famous
knight in the whole world." Actually the chapter represents a
futile involvement with fear, superstition, and fantasy. It also
provides a measure of pure comic relief (and at the same time
grants insight into the melancholic nature which cannot laugh at
itself, for Don Quixote's self-image is clearly threatened by
Sancho's jibes). The folly is intensified when Don Quixote wins
Mambrino's helmet, a brass barber's basin, which represents another act of lawlessness in the name of chivalry.

But his separation from the social structure of which he is a
part reaches its apex in the freeing of the galley slaves. Through
this act he defies social order—would, in fact, turn it upside down
and loose the criminal element in society as he has loosed chaos
within himself. The distorted reference of this individual to his
group is never more clearly seen than in this episode. As a result
of it, Don Quixote and Sancho are attacked by the very slaves
they have freed and become fugitives before the Holy Brotherhood. This time they are forced to withdraw, whereas previously
they had withdrawn among the goatherds voluntarily.

It is this retirement with its parallel in the retirement of Cardenio which represents the psychological turning point of the work, for it is here that Don Quixote's ultimate defeat begins to emerge. He pretends he is mad like Amadis of Gaul, admitting that a knight may turn mad for no reason at all. When he admits that he is playing a role, merely repeating the experience of Amadis of Gaul (for the sake of repetition), we may see his downfall. For in his pride in the trappings and customs of the knight-errant, he has temporarily forgotten his central purpose. In acting *as if* he were mad, he substitutes a bookish role for idealistic action. Cardenio's penance is likewise a wasteful and meaningless one. Instead of attempting to cope with reality, Cardenio weeps futilely in the Sierra Morena. These two situations represent a kind of nadir of human behavior and a rescue is indeed in order, a rescue initiated from without.

Chapters 23 through 27 contain, then, the climax or nadir of the work (see Casalduero) if the novel is interpreted on the basis of the developing psychological pattern outlined in this introduction, for maximum psychological tension is achieved when the real world and the ideal world become polarities as they do in Don Quixote's penance in the mountains. Reality is here replaced by fantasy. In the episode with the galley slaves Don Quixote is still interacting (if mistakenly) with his society. A turning point is reached, however, when society is rejected for the fantasy world of Amadis of Gaul. Don Quixote may, however, show a moment of sanity at the very heart of his insanity when he imitates the madness of Amadis (RIQ, 119-120), for the desire to *act* as a madman implies that one knows how a sane man acts. Furthermore, it is in this episode that he tells Sancho that Dulcinea is the daughter of Lorenzo Corchuelo. It is his only reference to Dulcinea as a peasant girl. And so in the depths of his dementia may be seen the seeds of his eventual recovery. Such is Cervantes' genius in handling the ambiguities of human behavior. The denouement of the novel begins with this scene after Don Quixote symbolically abandons his quest in the pointlessness of his behavior in the Sierra Morena and is rescued by the party headed by the curate and the barber.

The entire passage in which Don Quixote imitates Amadis

of Gaul also illustrates the author's skillful use of literary quotation, which is for Cervantes "far more than a mere ornament
attached to or imposed upon his novel with no organic connection" (ME, 60). As Herman Meyer demonstrates, in *Don Quixote*
the "'quotative life' is a form of life" (ME, 64-65) whereby
Cervantes produces the tension between the "lofty" and the
"lowly." The antithesis between the high and the low created by
the use of quotation balances the more obvious antithesis between illusion and reality in the book. Thus whereas in Rabelais
the quotation had served to enrich meaning and to support structure, in Cervantes' novel the quotation is "a direct and pure
expression of meaning" (ME, 71), a rich elaboration of a basic
antithesis of the novel.

Part IV, a section dealing with the resolving of problems
starting with Chapter 28, opens fittingly with the tale of Dorothea
(meaning gift of God), for Dorothea is a positive force in the
novel. Cervantes now turns to the figures around Don Quixote.
The various reconciliations, meetings, and meaningful involvements of the other characters in this part contrast sharply with
Don Quixote's lack of involvement. "The Tale of Foolish Curiosity" underlines the kind of play acting which has forced Don
Quixote into death in life and Anselmo and Lothario into death
itself.

The structure of Part IV is punctuated by five digressions:
(1) "The Tale of Foolish Curiosity," (2) the conversation on arms
and letters, (3) the Captive's tale, (4) Don Quixote's conversation
with the canon, and (5) the tale of Anselmo and Eugenio. The
progression of this unit is orderly, illustrating the polarity between
involvement and withdrawal and leading from Don Quixote's
rescue by Dorothea to the imprisonment on the wagon. In Part IV
we find a more rapid alternation between involvement and withdrawal, although it is the same pattern which has characterized
the preceding sections, both of which end in the hero's retreat.
Thus the author follows Dorothea's active participation in Don
Quixote's rescue which he juxtaposes with the pointless curiosity
of Anselmo; he contrasts Don Quixote's battle with the wineskins
with the meaningful reconciliations of the two couples; Don
Quixote's abstract discourse on arms and letters seems empty

beside the active involvement of the Captive; the shackling of Don Quixote's arm or his power is followed by a frenzied misuse of power—the *mêlée* over the recovery of Mambrino's helmet. Don Quixote's imprisonment on the wagon, his conversation with the canon, and the tale of Anselmo and Eugenio all forebode the final withdrawal of the hero. Before this happens, however, Don Quixote makes one final sally against rainmakers, against those who would bring about fertility and new life. Clearly the involvements of the hero in this final section symbolize the sterile outcome of his quest.

This counterpoint may be examined more closely. Dorothea's rescue of Don Quixote is part of a larger rescue she accomplishes, that of her relationship to Don Ferdinand. A lesser woman reacting to rejection by her lover would have retired to a convent. Instead Dorothea, with intelligence and good humor, presses her case until Don Ferdinand is forced to yield to the justice of her demands. Her rescue of Don Quixote is also the result of her ability to face reality, even the reality of a madman. By falling in with Don Quixote's fantasy as she has followed the mad wanderings of her lover, she is able to lure Don Quixote back to the inn and away from his solitary withdrawal from people.

A different situation is represented by Anselmo's foolish curiosity. Although to all appearances Anselmo is happily married to Camilla, he cannot help but meddle with his lot. Whereas Dorothea is devoted to the cause of meaningful reconciliation, Anselmo plays wanton and dangerous games with his wife as pawn, withdrawing from a purposeful existence with her.

In Don Quixote's battle with the wineskins, we find the hero engaged with an inanimate object which he takes for a giant, whereas in the reunions of Cardenio and Lucinda, of Don Ferdinand and Dorothea, we see human beings involved with other human beings and confusions set straight.

Furthermore, the talk of arms and letters takes on the aura of the university debate, of the ivory tower, when seen in the light of the Captive's tale which follows. The Captive is an active participant in life; he spends little time discoursing about its abstract nature.

But when, two chapters later, Don Quixote is tied up by the

arm by two prostitutes, his captivity is quite different from that of
the Captive. The latter had been *freed* by a woman whereas Don
Quixote has been shorn of his power by women. The *mêlée* which
occurs the next day illustrates the kind of crazy activity in which
Don Quixote's freedom always results. Unless he is restrained,
scenes occur filled with "shouts, screams, amazement, fear, alarm,
dismay, slashings, punches, blows, kicks and effusion of blood"
(407). In this final pair of episodes both the ridiculous and
pathetic character of Don Quixote's retreats and sallies become
fully apparent.

In summary it may be seen that Cervantes has skillfully
alternated participation and withdrawal in developing Don Quixote's madness. The mistaken involvements of the Don in the first
three parts lead to two major withdrawals from the world into
the solitude of nature, one voluntary and one to escape arrest.
The fourth part continues to deal with the polarity between
withdrawal and participation but in a different way. Don Quixote
has achieved the ultimate withdrawal through his passive credulity
and contrasts with those around him who are engaged, as are Dorothea and the Captive, in constructive courses of action. Cervantes,
in the 1605 *Quixote,* shows how the credulity of the hero in his
literal rendering of books of chivalry is a credulity which in the
end will be turned against him by others. Don Quixote has moved
in the 1605 novel through a series of attempts to right matters in
the world, to tackle giants and whole armies, to rescue maidens
in distress, to set straight social wrongs to a point where as a
knight in distress he has been rescued by a maiden (Dorothea)
and is now manipulated by the very fantasies which have inspired
his active quest to reestablish the world of chivalry.

Yet it is important to recognize, although Don Quixote has
met defeat and failure at every turn, that his idealisms persist. For
as José Antonio Maravall shows in his book on the humanism of
arms, Cervantes' intentions must be seen in the light of the spiritual and intellectual tradition to which he was heir. Thus the
practice of arms, as the chapter on arms and letters indicates, was
for the later Middle Ages and the Renaissance a means of attaining an interior nobility, a spiritual (not merely physical) activity
through which bravery in upholding justice and in fulfilling one's

responsibilities was acquired. Therefore, although the trappings of the chivalric romance are continually parodied by Cervantes, the practice of arms is considered to be a more serious matter, closely linked to the reform of man, society, and the state. This hope for reform, which characterized the thought of Erasmus and the late medieval cultural tradition, had by Cervantes' time been badly tarnished, although not entirely abandoned. For *Don Quixote* is not finished; a third expedition is hinted at in the final pages of the 1605 book. The ambiguity of the hero, then, results partly from the two traditions from which Cervantes creates him. It is Don Quixote's fresh resolve, his continual inner fidelity to his ideal, even to the point of a third sally, that suggests a real participation and involvement in arms despite the fact that his actions again and again neutralize and even deny his idealisms, forcing him to retreat eventually in a cage to his home.

III.

Whereas the emphasis in the 1605 *Quixote* has been on Don Quixote's fluctuating relationship to his society in his attempt to revive chivalry (ending in the necessity of his withdrawing from that society), the 1615 *Quixote* stresses Don Quixote's discovery of himself. Many of the other characters in this volume act as mirrors to reflect the hero from different angles. As Ortega y Gasset points out in speaking of Goethe, "human life is made up of the problem of itself" ("In Search of Goethe from Within," *New Partisan Reader 1945-1953*, p. 296.) It is not, in other words, a confrontation with obstacles in the world outside of oneself or with something that already *is*. Cervantes and Don Quixote may have learned this through their encounters in the 1605 book where Don Quixote engages in battle with a series of "things"—windmills, a herd of sheep, or wineskins. The entire motion of the 1615 *Quixote* is reflexive and inward rather than outward—seeking, as it were, the well-springs of human action and behavior. For example, Don Quixote's first encounter in the 1605 *Quixote* is with the farmer and Andrew; his first quest in the 1615 *Quixote* is in search of Dulcinea, a being who has no existence outside of Don Quixote's own imagination. To seek her is to seek himself. Cervantes recognizes that the wise man makes sure of his own identity before he undertakes to modify or change the ways of others. Don Quixote seems partially to understand this point when he says to the barber "I . . . am not Neptune, and I am not trying to make anyone believe me wise when I am not. . . . I am only at pains to convince the world of its error" (477). Don Quixote knows who he is not, but not until the end of the 1615 book does he know who he is.

In fact, as Mia Gerhardt (GER, 52) shows, the play of mirrors becomes in this part so complicated, the confusion Cervantes creates between reality and illusion, between life and books becomes so complete, that the reader is likely to lose himself. The confusion is compounded not only by the fact that the two parts of the *Quixote* comment on one another, but we now have the imposter *Quixote* of Avellaneda with which to contend. By incorporating one of Avellaneda's characters (Don Alvaro Tarfe), Cervantes finally eliminates this alien element by giving it a life within the original book and creating from an illusion still another illusion.

Cervantes divided the 1615 edition of *Quixote* into four sections, which provide Don Quixote with many mirrors in which to view himself. The first seven chapters serve as a means of getting the third expedition under way. Chapters 8 through 29 offer varied and contrasting views of the hero as he is reflected by others who meet him. The next twenty-seven chapters (30 through 57) deal with the series of humiliations at the castle of the Duke and Duchess, depriving both master and squire of any identity as such and indicating the emptiness of their existence at this stage. The final seventeen chapters (57 through 74) show Don Quixote gradually assuming his true identity. A more detailed discussion of these four main sections will indicate the way in which Cervantes handles the problem of acquiring self-knowledge.

It is fitting that the Prologue to the 1615 book should concern the imposter writer and his sequel to the 1605 *Quixote* because the sham *Don Quixote* is, of course, a kind of mirror image basic to the entire volume. Presumably it attests continually to the worth and authenticity of the original and is never far from Cervantes' thoughts throughout the 1615 book.

The first seven chapters introduce the major theme, the mirroring and discovery of self that is to be fully developed as the novel progresses. The priest and barber reappear in Chapter 1, one month after the end of the first part, and revive the theme of chivalric madness as they chat with Don Quixote, for these two characters had been and still are secretly drawn to Don Quixote's mad fantasy themselves. To open the 1615 *Quixote* with the very two who had "rescued" him in the 1605 book creates an ironic mirror image of the hero. A more central mirror image in the 1615 story is the bachelor, Sampson Carrasco, who is introduced in Chapter 3. Sampson also yearns to be a knight errant but for different reasons from those of Don Quixote, reasons which prove to be mainly self-centered. It is Sampson who becomes Knight of the Mirrors, and it is later Sampson who effects the denouement of the novel by unhorsing Don Quixote. In both encounters he reflects and foils the hero. And finally in Chapter 5, the scene between Sancho and his wife mirrors scenes that take place between Don Quixote and Sancho, for Sancho plays Don Quixote with his wife, who plays Sancho with him. In these ways the opening chapters establish the mode of the 1615 *Quixote*.

In the second section of the book (Chapters 8-29), we view a number of characters who also reflect Don Quixote. As we have pointed out, Don Quixote seeks Dulcinea (but he is really seeking himself, for she is a creation of his own imagination). He finds her as a peasant girl, fallen from her ass, ugly, low, and stinking of raw garlic. Although Don Quixote does not recognize his own image, he too has often fallen from his mount and his appearance too is less appealing than that of characters like Amadis of Gaul. He is forced to invoke enchanters to explain the appearance of Dulcinea; never does he see his own image in the mirror that Dulcinea provides.

Two kinds of 'players' next occupy the attention of the knight, complementing his own kind of play acting. First, there is the wagon of players and then the Knight of the Mirrors whose title makes him a key figure in the 1615 book. Among the actors on the wagon is a knight who wears a plumed hat rather than a

helmet, suggesting that his role is not a militant one. Once again
Don Quixote's vision is blurred, and he fails to see himself in this
knight. Had he looked, he might have seen that his own costume
bore a resemblance to that of the actor and that like him, he was
borne on the 'wagon of death.' Yet these "phantoms," as he names
them, make him uncomfortable, and he wishes to leave them
in search of "more substantial adventures" (538). Had he been
able to discern the ineffectiveness of his own actions, that is, the
phantomlike quality in himself, he could have made his own life
more purposeful. The actors show him a likeness which is too
close to truth for comfort. He tells Sancho that plays hold up the
mirror to us at every step (539), but still he fails to look into this
mirror when it is thrust before him.

Likewise the Knight of the Mirrors offers Don Quixote the
opportunity of viewing his own image. But Don Quixote never
perceives that the ambiguous motives of Carrasco are similar to
his own. That is, Sampson Carrasco's motives are both philanthropic and frivolous. Don Quixote's vision is philanthropic; his
means of carrying out his vision is frivolous. But Quixote does
not grasp the full import of Sampson's defeat—that philanthropic
goals are best achieved by less frivolous means, and he sends
Sampson off to El Toboso firmly convinced that he will go.

The episodes seem to go in groups and pairs in this section
of the book, providing a complex pattern of reciprocal commentary on one another and on Don Quixote. Thus in the preceding
set of episodes we are able to contrast three kinds of actors: the actor of the stage, the prankster, and the amateur actor of knight-
errantry. The stage actor is involved in a double existence and,
therefore, is dismissed by Don Quixote as a phantom. The prankster's purposes are partly selfish ones, like those of the phantom
actors ineffectual in achieving creative ends. Don Quixote, living
the role he has chosen day and night, is unaware of his double
existence. His purposes are unselfish ones, but because he has
deceived himself and has denied his identity, he too is phantomlike in his effect upon the world which he would save.

The connection between Cervantes' treatment of play acting
and the concept of *theatrum mundi* should be noted here. Cervantes wrote with full awareness that he was following a tradition

which by the seventeenth century had become almost a literary cliché—"all the world's a stage." Cervantes' knowledge of this tradition makes significant the whole question of role in *Don Quixote* and the whole vexing problem of Don Quixote's attitude toward his own way of life. It is as if Cervantes, having grasped the full significance of *theatrum mundi,* the purposeful and successful staging of one's life in making order out of unordered experience, had turned his parody on this tradition, also. He shows us in Don Quixote a misguided player on the stage of life, making *dis*order out of order, unable to direct his own play or to act in it. Thus the actors who are seen as "phantoms" are at the same time more substantial than Don Quixote; and the puppets whom he destroys more purposeful than his destruction of them. If Don Quixote is aware of his "role," it is in terms of what he considers his ability to formulate and order his own life, an ability which Cervantes shows us he sadly and tragically lacks.

The Gentleman in Green and the lions in their cages, the subjects of the next two episodes, are also curiously similar and dissimilar to Don Quixote. In fact, the episode of the lions is intercalated within the encounter with Don Diego, so that Cervantes may say that Don Diego is somewhat like the lion who sleeps when the door to his cage is opened and freedom or a challenge is offered. It will be readily remembered that Don Quixote also has been confined in a cage. Yet when the door was opened, he took advantage of his opportunity to go free, to engage in new adventures. By contrast, the Gentleman in Green remains in his village prudently avoiding any steps which might lead to active confrontation with others. Don Diego, on another level, is a mirror image of Alonso Quixada whom Don Quixote is to find at the end of his adventures. Therefore, Don Quixote might have been able to see his image in both animal and man. What differentiates them is their attitudes toward the cages in which they are confined. The lion and Don Diego are unaware of their opportunities for freedom ("the lion lay down again in his cage with great calmness and composure") (576); Don Quixote has *created* his freedom to act as a knight-errant. Were he able to look into the mirror offered him here, he would find encouragement for his quest in the behavior of Don Diego, and yet, like

Don Diego, he himself is not using his potentiality to the best possible end.

The succeeding adventures concerning Camacho's wedding and the visit to Montesinos' cave involve two love affairs, both of which parallel and contrast with the relation of Don Quixote to Dulcinea. Basilio's aims are earthly ones; Don Quixote's transcend physical love. Durandarte, on the other hand, a product of Don Quixote's imagination, is transfixed on his bier, his heart in the possession of the lady Belerma. Don Quixote, in descending into Montesinos' cave has descended, as it were, into his own unconscious world. Durandarte may thus stand for Don Quixote's repressed knowledge of self; enchanted as he is by his mad fantasy, he is no more effective in dealing with life than the transfixed Durandarte; like Durandarte's, Don Quixote's heart has been cut from his chest and lies in the possession of a maiden no more real than the Lady Belerma. Yet Don Quixote has the potential to rise from his bier and to assume an effective role were he able to see himself in his own fantasy of the enchanted Durandarte and able to put into constructive action the idealism embodied in his love for Dulcinea. Basilio, of course, contrasts sharply with both Durandarte and Don Quixote. Basilio's aims are confined to the winning of a wife. Furthermore, he knows who he is, and he is resourceful in achieving his ends. Although he lacks the idealisms of Don Quixote (he is advised by Don Quixote to give up his tricks), his heart has not been separated from his body as both Don Quixote's and Durandarte's have. Don Quixote's knighthood is not trickery, although it may be viewed as a means of accomplishing his ends by "playing a role." Thus Basilio, Durandarte, and Don Quixote all throw light upon each other, contrasting with one another in a myriad of ways. Through such mirroring devices Cervantes offers his hero the possibility of self-knowledge.

Cervantes indicates the growing deterioration of Don Quixote as knight in the following two episodes. He uses an ape and asses to represent the abasement of Don Quixote, for the Renaissance reader considered both animals "funny" (RUS, 321). The ape and Master Peter, who speak with one voice and thus are in a sense synonymous, both contrast and compare with Don Quixote. In the episode of the galley slaves Master Peter had behaved little better than an ape in his unreasoning anger at the very man who had helped him. By contrast Don Quixote considers loyalty among the highest of the virtues he proclaims, However, Don Quixote himself behaves little better than an ape in destroying another's property, the puppets of Master Peter. In fact, the scene in which we see the aging knight rain furious blows upon the "puppet-heathenry" is reminiscent of the senseless rage of an angry ape in captivity. Once again the central contrast lies in the difference in intention. Don Quixote's intentions always lack self-centeredness. He attacks the puppets because he thinks he is helping fugitives; Master Peter's motives, on the contrary, have been selfish ones. Recognizing Don Quixote's madness, Master Peter has made no allowances for it, stoning him because he has been asked to present himself before Dulcinea del Toboso, although he had been helped by the Don. Master Peter, therefore, serves as both foil and mirror for Don Quixote. Cervantes implies that if one's means of achieving ends are mistaken, then the ends are likely to be no better than those of a common criminal. On the other hand, Don Quixote, unlike Master Peter, pays for his destruction.

The disagreement and yet essential agreement between Unamuno and Ortega y Gasset is nowhere better illustrated than in their opinions of the puppet show. Unamuno feels Don Quixote is exonerated and ennobled by his payment for the damage he has done. Unamuno further apotheosizes him with a suggestion that Cervantes sees Don Quixote here as a symbolic revolutionary, a much-needed reformer of the Spanish parliament which in this scene he, in effect, would reduce to splinters (UN, 204). On the contrary, Ortega, who judges Don Quixote both mad and harmful, finds the scene an opportunity to discourse on the relation of poetry and reality and shows that through Don Quixote's dementia and simple-mindedness "emanations come and go from one continent to the other" (ORT, 134). The special value of criticism in Spanish, which identifies Don Quixote as a national hero, must not be overlooked. It is well symbolized in the group of statues dedicated to Cervantes in the Plaza de España in Madrid. Here in bronze, Don Quixote, followed by Sancho, may be seen as knight and crusader, hand outstretched in a gesture of victory, lance uplifted and erect. Above him in marble towers the seated figure of his creator and on either side sit his women—Dulcinea on his right; Aldonza Lorenzo on his left. Both Unamuno and Ortega, each in his own way, interpret and pay homage to such an image.

But to return to the text—as Master Peter is a prototype of his ape, so the villagers are prototypes of their asses, traditionally far stupider than apes. Both villager and ass can bray, and it is against a background of brayers that Don Quixote is now viewed. The villagers, whether aldermen or bailiffs, have debased themselves to the level of asses. Even their banners carry images of open-mouthed asses. Don Quixote's advice to the brayers is advice he might well have taken himself. He tells them, "whoever takes them [arms] up for trifles or for matters laughable . . . is, in my opinion, lacking in all common sense" (650). Yet he himself has only recently taken up arms against a stage full of puppets. Once again he is mirrored in the people he confronts. Hardly brighter than the asses that they imitate, the brayers, thinking Sancho is mocking them, run master and squire out of town. Yet the purposes of both are peaceable by comparison with those of the contentious villagers who are ready to fight at the slightest provocation, almost for the sake of fighting. Cervantes shows us that Don Quixote may be both the image and antithesis of the brayers and their asses as well as of Master Peter and his ape. In fact, the pairs themselves suggest a grotesque mockery of Don Quixote and Sancho as a pair. Cervantes concludes this second section of the 1615 *Quixote* with Don Quixote more debased and moving further and further away from what he thinks he is. Only when the real and the ideal are reunited will Don Quixote have discovered his identity.

In the final episode with the enchanted boat, Don Quixote's identity reaches its nadir, in his defeat by a nonhuman force, the mill-race. It is a fitting forerunner of the coming encounter with the Duke and the Duchess where the Don's identity is submerged in yet another way.

Within the third section (Chapters 30-57) of the 1615 novel, Don Quixote has ceased to exist in his own right, but through a series of humiliations and degradations has become a toy in the hands of his host and hostess, the Duke and Duchess. Likewise

Sancho is converted from a friend of the Don to a pawn of the Duke. The emptiness of both Don Quixote's and Sancho's existence is mirrored in the emptiness of the life of the Duke and Duchess and their court, although theirs is the emptiness of lives devoted to cruel practical jokes perpetrated at the expense of knight and squire. From the passive defense of the Countess Trifaldi on Clavileño to the attacks on Don Quixote by the cats and by the Duchess and Altisidora to his abortive fight with a lackey, Don Quixote is mocked, derided, and humiliated. Likewise Sancho's governorship is a means of derisive fun, ending in his encasement between two shields, like a tortoise in its shell. Sancho takes the first step in his own progress toward redemption when he recognizes the folly of his governorship; and Don Quixote takes his first step in finally eschewing openly his idleness amid the luxury at the castle. Yet the idleness of Don Quixote and Sancho is far less malignant than that of those who mock them.

Don Quixote at last discovers his true identity in the fourth and final section of the book following a series of total defeats. No longer the pawn of Duke and Duchess, he is forced to accept his defeats as completely his own. Trampled by bulls, defeated by the Knight of the White Moon, and trampled by hogs (the key episodes in this section), Don Quixote emerges through the fever of his final illness, cleansed of his mad fantasy. Meanwhile Sancho's self-flagellation provides a kind of humorous counterpoint for the Don's various tramplings.

Don Quixote's downfall is predicted in yet another way in these final episodes—by the actual violence which is introduced. Claudia Jeronima's fatal wounding of her lover, Roque Guinart's killing of a follower, the battle on the galley, all make Don Quixote's previous actions seem trivial by comparison. He becomes an onlooker even though on the galley a real opportunity to engage a traditional enemy of all knights—the Turks—is offered him (see RIQ, 166).

And finally many of the episodes (especially the later ones) apart from Don Quixote's three most disastrous encounters in Part IV, are repetitive episodes reflecting events in other sections of the book or making the same points. Thus the spurious second part of Don Quixote, written by Avellaneda, is mentioned again during Don Quixote's visit to the printer's shop; Don Antonio (although more cynical in his passive malevolence) reflects the Duke in Part III; the enchanted head has the same function as Master Peter's ape in Part II; and Anna Felix brings to mind Zoraida in the 1605 book. Furthermore, for two chapters Don Quixote actually returns to the castle of the Duke and Duchess. This repetition, linking the final episodes of the book to earlier episodes, provides a unity and sense of return which mirrors Don Quixote's own return to his village and to himself.

The image at last perceived in the pool is that of Alonso Quixano the Good. Don Quixote's eyes are opened to his own likeness at the moment when they are about to be closed in death. Thus Cervantes, through a skillful interweaving of theme and structure, establishes the immortality of his hero, who is involved in the search of Everyman for his fellow humans and for himself. For as Maravall shows (MAR, 164), Don Quixote is attempting not to defeat others but to recreate himself through the practice of arms. Thus his discovery of an identity in these final pages suggests an apprenticeship to a *true* chivalry, not to a false one of exterior forms. A nobility of spirit has been acquired, an interiorized virtue, suggested by his new title—Alonso Quixano the Good.

Don Quixote, 1605

Prologue

Cervantes' insistence throughout the novel that he is a "step-father," that is, not the real father, of his book is similar in essence to the Greek author's invocation of the Muse or to the concept of the divine origin of genius. He may also, of course, have taken his stand as a political dodge shifting any responsibility for unorthodox points of view to Cide Hamete. Even more likely, we find here Renaissance man defining his God-given gift. To bear out this assumption we find Don Quixote's remark to the Gentleman in Green in the 1615 *Quixote:* "the poet is born—I mean the natural poet comes out of his mother's womb and, with that impulse which Heaven has given him, without further study or art, composes things which prove the truth of the saying: 'There is a god in us' " (569). It is not coincidence that this type of invocation appears on the first page of the Prologue.

* * *

The satire on other writers (especially Lope de Vega, OB, 11) which follows, sets the tone for a large part of the book; it points a critical finger at various fields of endeavor, particularly literature. Cervantes uses the two means, that of evoking a Renaissance muse and that of satirizing contemporary writing, which start off the Prologue, to present two basic themes of the book—genius (spirit) and the need to employ genius in a meaningful way. Furthermore, in the Prologue the words of wisdom come from "a friend," not didactically from Cervantes. The inner Cervantes speaks through others and establishes many alter-egos. The book is full of various projections.

* * *

Cervantes' purpose is, he tells us, "invective against books of chivalry." Another purpose is, of course, to portray his hero, "the chastest lover and most valiant knight," that is, to set forth inner values and to show how these values must bear some meaningful relation to outer reality. Cervantes establishes in the Prologue his protest against an abstract value system and his argument for a synthesis of spirit and body, of inner and outer man, of Don Quixote and of Sancho Panza.

Chapter 1

The point must be made at the very beginning of the discussion that the source of Don Quixote's madness, the reading of too many books of chivalry, is also the source of the reality of Don Quixote's exploits. For if literature is merely a representation of life, then Don Quixote's life of knight-errantry, which *imitates* the life of knights in books, must be real. At the same time literature has its own reality, for it produces the illusions and idealisms which form the significant matter of any man's life. Such paradoxes form the substance of *Don Quixote* (PRE).

However, Cervantes soon makes it clear that books of chivalry, to which we are introduced in this chapter, are the butt of his biting and yet funny irony. Thus he parodies the style of Feliciano de Silva on the first page by means of the quotation of a ridiculous sentence from one of his works. All these ways in which the literature of chivalry is used, then, give an indication of the subtleties with which Cervantes worked and which this study will attempt to unravel. The very object of Cervantes' parody is at the same time the means through which he establishes a value system and the means by which he produces a sense of reality for his novel. Such are the multivalent and multileveled meanings which Cervantes gives *Don Quixote*.

* * *

Although *Don Quixote* may be an invective against books of chivalry, it does not follow, of course, that it is an invective against the values of chivalry. It is not the true practice of arms, which was seen by Renaissance man as an exercise for the cultivation of the chivalric virtues, that Cervantes deplores, but its false application, the ivory tower of chivalric poses. Thus Cervantes directed his satire at all the empty ritual of the chivalric mode, a ritual which in many books of chivalry had become an end in itself. The ritual ridiculed in this chapter is of this nature: Don Quixote's niece rather than the knightly nephew, the paste-board visor to replace a metal one, the farm girl, Aldonza (a name signifying vulgarity) instead of Queen Guinevere, and fifteenth-century armor worn in seventeenth-century Spain. Furthermore, Don Quixote's madness is not the result of unrequited passion but of reading too many books of chivalry—a knight gone mad ironically from a truly Platonic love. Even the fact that the place where Don Quixote lives in La Mancha is unnamed burlesques the exotic names of kingdoms of the chivalric romances. Moreover, a great deal of uncertainty exists about the exact form of Quixada's own name (RIQ, 77-79). Cervantes does not definitely establish the names of other main characters also to satirize the pseudo-historical tendencies of writers of chivalric romances. In some instances, however, he is entirely clear about geographical locations and names of persons to give a sense of truth to a book which must at the same time continually be viewed through its ironic intent.

Leo Spitzer in "Perspectivism in *Don Quixote*" suggests another reason Cervantes did not establish names definitely by reference to what he calls "literary perspectivism." That is, medieval etymology (SP, 47) often proposed many sources for the same word to account for various meanings God may have deposited in a word. A word then not only conveyed the correspondence between it and what it represented but also a mystery making this correspondence uncertain. Also medieval etymology indicated that the world, as it is given to man, is susceptible to many explanations. Furthermore, changes in name offered various possible vantage points from which to view a character and were common practice in the Old and New Testaments and of interest to ancient philology. The change of name at baptism was imitated in medieval chivalry by the change of name at the dubbing of the knight (SP, 50). The importance given to changes in names was derived, then, from the various interpretations which such a change provided, even to revealing God's mysteries.

* * *

An understanding of how Cervantes transmuted reality in *Don Quixote* is essential to grasping the meaning of the book. The costume and other props that Don Quixote adopts in this chapter transform reality in order that he may deceive others and thereby carry out his mission in the practice of arms. Later he sees things, for example, the windmills, as they are not, thus deceiving himself. Reality is thereby doubly transformed; others are deceived about him, and he is deceived about others. The hero becomes both the deceiver and the deceived. Cervantes adopted the whole theme of false appearances, of a deceptive world, as Maravall suggests, from the ascetic tradition of the Middle Ages, which stressed indifference or aversion to worldly things. By showing the shifting and unreliable nature of exterior reality, Cervantes is better able to stress the permanence of the values underlying the practice of arms as it was interpreted by the cultural tradition to which he was heir (MAR, 168-169).

Chapter 2

Rabelaisian humor was as important in Renaissance Spain as in most other countries in this age. Neither Cervantes nor Shakespeare ignored it. Dogberry's "Write me down an ass" is comparable to Don Quixote's mistaking two prostitutes for "maidens" in Chapter 2. Renaissance humor, like the age itself, often contrasts the real and the ideal. Thus the sudden juxtaposition of maidens and prostitutes sets off the laughter of the reader. Or in the example from *Much Ado About Nothing*, conscientious prosecution of a case and blundering stupidity are suddenly set side by side, to produce a ridiculous effect.

Chapter 3

Don Quixote is knighted at the beginning of his adventures. Actually Don Quixote could never really have been knighted, as Martín de Riquer points out (RIQ, 88), because he was insane, he was poor, and he was knighted inauthentically and in ridicule. And yet the rustics, the mentally unstable, the fools, Sancho (who was not present at the ceremony), and Don Quixote himself all take his knighthood seriously. The "educated" and the "noble," however, see through the farce. The establishment of this ambiguity early in the book lends the exact tone that Cervantes needs to convey a sense of the hybrid nature of reality which consists both of truth and illusion. Just where the line between the two can be drawn is never clear. As Don Quixote's niece later says, "and, worst of all . . . you're a knight when you aren't" (505).

* * *

The innkeeper accepts Don Quixote's fantasy for a while partly to humor him, partly because he, like many of the characters Don Quixote meets, was himself captivated by chivalric lore. Neither innkeeper nor Don is able to come to terms with the conflicting desires within him. Perhaps, says Cervantes, more people would be better people if they were able to recognize the knights within them.

Perhaps Don Quixote would be a better person, if, as the innkeeper suggests, he carried a purse, some clean shirts, and a box of ointments. Sorcerers, he tells Don Quixote, are not always reliable as bearers of aid, nor are prayers to Dulcinea capable of warding off death and danger. But the medieval writer of chivalric tales erected such fantastic protectors against man's ancient enemies. The Renaissance tells us that a few practical precautions will serve as well, even better perhaps. But it does not neglect to tell us also that a clean shirt and a box of ointment are not in themselves sufficient. To what purposes we use our lives after they have been saved is the point to which *Don Quixote* is directed. The book is in this sense another Perceval legend with a hero whose real quest is for the meaning of human existence—the search, in fact, of the entire Renaissance.

Ironically, the innkeeper is forced into foregoing payment for Don Quixote's lodging, almost proving Don Quixote's own point that as a knight he does not have to pay for his visit to a "castle." The innkeeper's motive is, of course, not to honor a knight but to be rid of his guest. The higher practicality of preserving the reputation and his inn overrides the minor consideration of cost of board and lodging. An intelligent and shrewd practicality.

Chapter 4

Cervantes points out the flaw in Don Quixote's whole plan in the episode of Andrew and his master, although even Don Quixote's mistakes, his unconscious goals, are in harmony with his avowed aims. For example, in figuring seven reals for nine months at 73 reals (incorrectly amended to 63 in editions after the first, RIQ, 89), he favors Andrew rather than the farmer. But noble as his ideal of redressing wrongs is, his means of implementing it is futile and impotent, even dangerous. Thus, he expects the farmer to honor the oath of knighthood, an external aspect of chivalry, rather than the spirit of the oath, which should survive. Don Quixote confuses these two levels of reality. Because of the farmer's horse and stave he assumes him to be a knight, although this farmer is not a knight in any way, even in spirit. What Cervantes says again and again is that identity cannot be established by appearances; Don Quixote's pasteboard visor and his lance are not what make up the knight within him.

For the humanist a man must be in harmony with his society, as well as with himself. Don Quixote, who is oriented only inwardly, is constantly running across people who are oriented only outwardly. Thus the farmer resumes his beating of Andrew as soon as Don Quixote is out of sight; for him, as for the innkeeper in the earlier scene, appearance and reputation are prime considerations. Cervantes shows that these illusions created purposely for selfish ends are in reality far more destructive than Don Quixote's relatively harmless fantasies created for society's benefit. This farmer has no principles to defend; Don Quixote has. Gradually one becomes aware that Don Quixote in his madness is probably more sane than the majority of people he meets.

Chapter 5

In the following episode Don Quixote meets merchants from Toledo. He demands that they declare Dulcinea the most beauteous maiden in the world, sight unseen. When they ask to see a picture lest they perjure themselves, Don Quixote insists they must maintain her beauty without seeing her. That this episode results in the first of Don Quixote's many beatings is not simply coincidence. In his demand he has completely separated appearance and reality, ideal and real, inner and outer man. He asks the merchants to swear to a truth of which there is no proof for them. He asks of them blind faith. His beating in a sense serves to reunite soul and body because with his shattered body he discovers it is impossible for him to rise without the assistance of a laborer who passes by. But the lesson does not sink in, for shortly thereafter, when he is addressed as Master Quixada, he flies into a rage and claims he is all the Twelve Peers of France and all the Nine Worthies wrapped in one. "I know who I am" (54)—an assertion of identity which is valid to society only when credentials and picture accompany it. To ask of other men blind faith in one's own inner world, a faith given by neither the merchants nor the laborer, is to try to usurp the role of God. Identity in this world is established by works. Don Quixote's beating only temporarily unites him with the humanistic world of interaction of human efforts.

A curious variation on Don Quixote's monomania appears in this chapter. He imagines the laborer who rescues him to be the Marquis of Mantua and himself to be the wounded knight, Baldwin. A little later on the way to the village, he takes himself for the captive Moor Abenarrage and the laborer for his captor, Rodrigo de Narvaez (characters in a tale by Montemayor.) These imagined roles fortify, through unconscious wish fulfillment, both Alonso Quixada and Don Quixote. The Marquis of Mantua is *uncle* to Baldwin. Although Don Quixote has supplied himself with charger and lady, he has not found the protection of the traditional uncle king of whom he is, in his current predicament, in great need. Furthermore, by transforming a laborer into a Marquis, he endows La Mancha (sounding like Mantua) with a nobleman whom it cannot in reality claim. Once astride the ass, however, his rescue having been accomplished, he can best rationalize his defeat by seeing himself as a famous captive, even though a Moor, in the hands of a governor of great wealth. For after all, what chance would a Moor be likely to have against the superior power of a Don Rodrigo? It is the same motive which causes him to see himself as Reynaldo of Montalban at the mercy of the famous Roland (armed with the trunk of an oak) at the beginning of Chapter 7 when his library is being looted.

Martín de Riquer points out that Cervantes probably borrowed parts of this episode from a play by an anonymous writer, *Entremos de los romances* (ca. 1588-1591). Here a hero, after being soundly beaten, remembers the romance of the Marquis of Mantua, reciting the same verses Quixote does (RIQ, 92-93). What is interesting, however, is the way Cervantes adds dimension to his source The simple buffoonery of the original is turned by Cervantes into symbolic complexities which serve to further his central theme—the confusion of reality and illusion.

Don Quixote would be at home in the world of the *symbolist,* for whom form is important. The imagination of the symbolist creates the world about him. Thus, Quixote's visor may be pasteboard—it is still a visor; a helmet may be a barber's basin. Yet Don Quixote's symbols never succeed in creating his ideal world, for their real meaning is understood by no one but himself. It is a solitary world, and the images he uses do not necessarily relate to others' experience. For the Renaissance, a system of medieval symbolism was empty of meaning and alogical. Don Quixote can be justified from a medieval point of view, but not by the humanistic culture in which Cervantes situates him.

Chapters 6 and 7

Of some importance is the fact that Cervantes' chapters in *Don Quixote* flow into one another. Therefore, it is often necessary, as will be seen in the discussions of chapters which follow, to include material from a preceding or a following chapter as well as sometimes, as with Chapters 6 and 7, to discuss two chapters together. Raymond S. Willis in *The Phantom Chapters of the "Quijote"* develops an interesting theory on Cervantes' divisions. He suggests that Cervantes is radically ahead of his generation in producing a new conception and treatment of time in literature. Each moment in life is for Cervantes not "a concluded entity" that stands before or after another moment but is instead "a condition of standing poised upon the circumstances of the past while thrusting forward into the not yet" (WP, 15). Thus the narrative often flows on without regard to chapter divisions, creating what we call the "novel"; for example, the story of the inquisition of the books in Chapter 6 is brought to a conclusion only in the middle of Chapter 7. The separation of chapters in *Don Quixote* is merely physical or formal, for the structure and rhythms, the verbal and thematic motifs, and the laws of syntax, as Willis shows, create stylistically a transcendent unity. The sense of anticlimax or bathos produced by the priest's final remark in Chapter 6 creates an "intensity of overflow" (WP, 37) or a tension to be resolved in the following chapter. Willis develops his thesis through discussions of "overflowing chapter-endings," "retrospective chapter-openings," and "pseudo-interruptions."

* * *

The inquisition held in Don Quixote's library by barber and priest may be read as a satire on censorship or on courts of justice, notably the inquisitorial courts of Cervantes' time. Reasons for suppressing a particular book have no rational basis. Some books are consigned to the barber's house to be read by no one until further judgment can be passed; some dealing with France are deposited in a dry well; one is saved because it was written by a king of Portugal, another because the author was a great friend of the priest. The methods are hit or miss—when the priest tires, a large number of books are cast out into the courtyard where the barber picks one at random that the priest declares must be saved. Furthermore, the priest shows extraordinary knowledge of and delight in the very library he is condemning, and so does the barber. Their knowledge of these books is such that they often suggest editing certain ones so that objectionable parts may be omitted—reference perhaps to certain inquisitorial punishments. One is tempted to ask if their wits may not have been touched, too, or, if these books are really the cause of Don Quixote's madness, why the priest and barber have escaped the malady. Surely wide reading has never been motivated by indifference or dislike. Meanwhile the niece and the housekeeper who have read none of the books are in favor of consigning the whole lot to the flames.

Scenes of social satire of the kind described above serve to relate the book to the times as well as to act as a foil to the pictures of the ideal world of knighthood envisioned by Don Quixote and by his books. We see in this chapter how the world often dispenses justice. Are Don Quixote's own methods any more unjust, we finally are forced to ask? Are not the madmen among us those with real vision? And who in the final analysis are the madmen? One thing is clear—that self-interest looms larger for both priest and barber than it ever does for Don Quixote. The barber acquires through the inquisition a good-sized library; the priest soon tires of his mission (Don Quixote never tires of his) and condemns the rest of the books sight unseen.

These chapters discussing the hero's first sally have a unity derived from the play *Entremos de los romances* (already noted) on which they were probably based. The burning of the books which caused the Don's disease should be a fitting conclusion to the first sally. However, a violent attack of madness, not a cure, follows the conflagration, and another expedition is born, this time with a neighbor, Sancho Panza, as squire. Cervantes is thus able to introduce the dialectic which forms the very foundation of the novel. A novel which attempts to unravel the truth of human experience and which is continually concerned, as all fiction must be, with both truth and the lie, has at its center both a dreamer and a man of the soil.

Chapter 8

Sancho and Don Quixote first disagree with each other over the matter of the windmills. The positions of the two are diametrically opposed at this point in the book. "What giants?" Sancho asks. And Don Quixote, forced finally to admit his error, falls back on the enchanters as an explanation. However, in books of chivalry battles with giants were described with such vividness (for example, the battle of Galaor with the giant in the first part of *Amadis of Gaul*) that it is little wonder Don Quixote's first case of hallucination concerns a giant(See RIQ, 98-100.) The symbolism here is of some interest. Windmills are the products of civilization in its search to harness and to utilize natural power. They symbolize, ironically, the very element which Don Quixote lacks. No humanistic reason, no windmill, that is, harnesses his powers. This symbol and Don Quixote's inability to recognize it provide in one chapter the whole novel in summary. Cervantes often presents in microcosm what elsewhere he may treat at great length. Don Quixote's violent attack on an image which represents control over chaos is also typical of what is occurring *within* his mind. His "giants" are often the ruling and controlling forces of society and are giants to no one but him. The Benedictine monks whom he attacks in the following scene represent the same basic symbol. To mistake the identity of these forces is to commit the gravest error possible for one dedicated to the pursuit of truth and justice. It is the common and often normal error of the adolescent. The adult learns, how-

ever, that one cannot combat that which one does not understand. *Don Quixote* is in one sense a novel of education, a
Bildungsroman in Spanish, for Don Quixote does become educated at the end.

*   *   *

Cervantes' humor bursts out from behind the cloud of Don
Quixote's error time and again. Sancho conveys a good part of
it, for the knight himself is often less laughable than pitiable,
thought-provoking, or melancholy for the twentieth-century
reader. Sometimes the humor involves delighted mockery of
other forms of writing or is sparked by exaggerations, as in the
fight in this chapter with the Basque, where the tension builds
with the description of the dreadful blows by which the warriors are about to annihilate one another, when the manuscript
(from which Cervantes is presumably copying) breaks off.

The best discussion of humor in *Don Quixote* is P. E. Russell's article, *"Don Quixote* as a Funny Book." Russell views the
humor from the point of view of the Renaissance reader. For
the Renaissance, madness, if not violent, was inseparable from
fun, for Cervantes and his contemporaries believed that laughter
was produced by some kind of ugliness. An Italian writer of the
period, Gian Giorgi Trissino, lists as funny: "an ugly or distorted
face, an inept physical condition, a silly word, a rough hand, an
unpleasant wine, a rose with a bad odor" (RUS, 321). Madness
(as seen in Don Quixote) and folly (as seen in Sancho) were the
twin faces of comedy.

Chapter 9

What about Cervantes' mythical manuscript and what about
the abrupt suspension of time while the author rummages around
and a number of weeks later, after a discovery and a translation, resumes? Why did Cervantes bother with the figment of

Cide Hamete Benengeli? First, there is the exotic tradition of the discovery of a manuscript of a Near-Eastern narrator which Cervantes used and sometimes mocked, as he did other literary traditions. It was common for books of chivalry to be based on works authors claimed to have translated under mysterious circumstances, so even the external structure of *Don Quixote* is in imitation of chivalric tales (RIQ, 102). Relying on Cide also enables Cervantes, who was writing in an Andalusian prison, to disclaim any statement which might offend the civil authorities.

In the 1615 *Quixote*, Don Quixote and Sancho accept Cide's history of them and testify against the accuracy of the imposter history. This indicates that somehow Cide was present but invisible throughout the 1605 *Quixote* and that he is still present but invisible in the later book. Cide himself, then, must be like one of Don Quixote's enchanters, invisible (but not, as many of them are, malign), for there is no indication of the physical presence of a third person. Cervantes seems to be saying through Cide that this enchanter is that god within us, that "genius" in himself, which he personfiies in this manner. Cide is more than a simple fictional device. He is Cervantes' means of defining genius, that which inspires and informs the work of the author. Through him Cervantes restates in his own way the classical, "Sing, Heavenly Muse." (All this is clearly indicated in Chapter 19 when Don Quixote asserts that Cide, the sage [genius], must have put into Sancho's thoughts the title Knight of the Sad Countenance.) The two travelers are well aware of their invisible companion and of their relationship to him.

That Don Quixote and Sancho know Cide's history to be the true one is positive proof of Cide's authorship, for who but the created would know their creator? In fact, Mia Gerhardt (GER, 35-39) makes a fascinating point on this subject. Since Don Quixote recreates the world according to his desire, he becomes in effect the author of the novel of which he is hero. The slightest suggestion of an independent creator (Cervantes himself) would have ruined the autonomy of Don Quixote. The invisible Cide thus serves Cervantes well in creating the illusion of truth, and this is what Cide means at the end of the 1615 book when he writes: "For me alone Don Quixote was born and I for him" (940). They are twin authors of the work.

*   *   *

Cervantes' pleasure in the mockery of literary devices is apparent in the lapse of time *between* Chapters 8 and 9. This lapse is so long and the warriors are left in such ludicrous postures until, in his desultory fashion, Cervantes runs across the second manuscript, that all suspense is drained from the situation, and the reader is hardened forever to this means of creating it.

In addition, Raymond Willis shows in *The Phantom Chapters of the "Quijote"* that the interruption of the combat between Don Quixote and the Basque is made all the more obvious because there has been no break in the text between the first and second sallies (WP, 88). Such interruptions are, therefore, Willis states, "logically self-nullifying," for they confirm their opposite, "textual liaison," (WP, 103) and thus reinforce Cervantes' dialectic between being and seeming. Since there is no real reason for interrupting the text where Cervantes chooses to do so, his interruptions recognize superficially the historical aspect of his work while at the same time they establish a fictional flow of events and of character.

Cervantes' strictly mechanical divisions coexist with the realism of everyday experience which knows no sharp demarcations. By blurring the divisions between chapters while at the same time retaining such divisions, Cervantes seems to adopt the historical viewpoint, which would see events as successive, and at the same time he establishes a new mode, that of modern fiction, the logic of which rests on a conception of the relativity of time.

The paradox of the ideal and the possible (which has been noted earlier in this text as well as by E. C. Riley in his book on Cervantes' aesthetics) is not the only basic paradox established by the author. A more important one for modern aesthetics is perhaps the paradox of the inner and outer worlds, of the flowing character of human experience as opposed to an ordered

Newtonian time sequence. It is through this paradox that Cervantes becomes the father of the modern novel.

Chapter 10

In the conversation between Sancho and his master in this chapter, we learn from Don Quixote that a single drop of the Balsam of Fierabras, will cure his ear. Sancho's lint and ointment are actually what he uses. Although herbs and dried fruits are a knight's ordinary fare, Don Quixote does not rule out other foods. Sancho never has to persuade Don Quixote to accept his point of view; Don Quixote comes to it after he has finished trying to persuade Sancho of his own view of reality. Lint and ointment are, after all, comforting by comparison with the Balsam of Fierabras. A fat chicken is, to be honest, tastier than dried herbs. Pursuit of the ideal is full of pain. An acceptance of nearby reality is easier and more expedient.

Chapter 11

At their first meal with the goatherds Sancho stands to serve Don Quixote. This is the only time in the book he follows such ceremony. Don Quixote informs him that knight errantry puts things all on equal footing. But more than these words, it is a change in their relationship that, as the book progresses, puts things on different footing. At this point in the story Sancho still sees Don Quixote as his master. Battles have not yet been forfeited nor fields ingloriously lost, nor is Sancho yet aware of Don Quixote's "madness." At the end of the 1615 book, during his governorship, Sancho becomes the kind of "master" he now imagines Don Quixote to be.

                              *   *   *

Is Cervantes so far ahead of his own time as to be able to gain perspective on the very essence of the Renaissance, to mock the concept of the noble savage, which had its source in this age of exploration? Its linking here with the order of knighthood, which sprang up (according to Don Quixote) to protect the maidens who needed no protection in earlier times, indicates that Cervantes sees through the "nobility" of savages as well as that of knights.

Chapter 12

The theme of thwarted love is introduced by the goatherd in the song of Olalla, whose mind is "framed of brass," yet who is leading her lover on. From here we move to the first digression, the story of Marcela who flings off all her lovers "like stones from a catapult." A digression within this digression pits Don Quixote against a fellow traveler, Vivaldo, on the way to Chrysostom's funeral. They argue over the relative virtues of two professions—knighthood and monkhood. Don Quixote defends knighthood on the grounds that a soldier must *carry out* what monks only pray for. The complexity of Don Quixote's deception is here apparent, also its Renaissance emphasis on action. But although he subscribes to the code of action, his deeds turn out to be empty forms, born of his diseased brain. The ideal, excellent though it may be, that is misdirected in practice, can be destructive. It is the direction of deeds, not the fact that they are deeds, that matters, and whether or not justice is executed depends on the performer. Don Quixote and Sancho are still ideologically far apart.

Chapters 13 and 14

Chapter 13 is a chapter of mockeries. Cervantes not only mocks the pastoral convention but the epic chapter opening and the Renaissance "garden in her face" lyric.

Don Quixote's idea that knights "endure more" than monks puts an emphasis on the virtue of suffering that is implicit in the entire chivalric code—stemming from the value the Christian ethic places on suffering. Vivaldo complains of knights' devotion to their mistresses instead of to God—not seeing this as a carry-over of the Christian devotion to Mary, Mother of God. In fact, the difference between monk and knight is simply a matter of form—the knight externalizing his inner world; the monk commenting on his consciousness from within—or praying. A knight's trappings may relate to his outer world within the framework of the romance, but Don Quixote's do not because he does not accept the outer world as his. Until his inner world can come to terms with windmills, he as well as his mission is lost.

The actual digression on Marcela and Chrysostom provides fitting parallels for the frame of mind in which we find Don Quixote at this point in the book. Although Marcela is ostensibly the culprit in the scene, she succeeds in showing us that she has established her identity, her inner world within an environment. Chrysostom, on the other hand, like Don Quixote, has been deluded by appearances. His inner world clashes with exterior reality, and he dies—giving the reader an early warning of the fate awaiting Don Quixote. As the episode ends, Don Quixote has intentions of offering to defend Marcela. Ironically Marcela, with her knowledge of self, needs no defence.

Marcela is no ideal figure, however. Her only virtue is her sense of identity: that her identity is hostile and antipathetic is a fact she has accepted. If Chrysostom is a parallel figure to Don Quixote, Marcela is anti-Quixotic: Don Quixote carries his illusions out into the world with missionary zeal; Marcela has no illusions and lacks social compassion. Rather than riding out into the world, she withdraws into the forest to contemplate her own image in the pools and lakes.

All of the later digressions, too, somehow comment on the main theme. Their pastoral nature is often mock pastoral. One way in which the mock pastoral element in this episode is brought out is through the arbitrary division made between goatherds and shepherds, that is, between the rustic man and the literary man. Although this separation does give us a "double vision" of the scene, it also comments on the comparative artificiality of the pastoral mode (RIQ, 105-106). The visions suggested by the main plot of *Don Quixote* are far more complex.

Marcela herself is a mock-shepherdess, for she spurns her flock. The Marcela episode provides a particularly brilliant foil for the main action. Again we ask, Which is the madman? (The name *Marcela* derives from the god of war, Mars. But Marcela's war, unlike Don Quixote's, is no holy one.)

Chapter 15

Sancho learns Falstaff's creed—"The better part of valour is discretion"—in the fight with the Yanguesans. He vows never again to fight peasant or knight and carries this resolve out in the majority of the remaining episodes. Don Quixote, in contrast, rationalizes, but it is a rationalization in keeping with all the others connected with his adoption of knighthood. Never again will he fight men who are not knights. It is interesting to note that Don Quixote sometimes is able to comment on his own madness and to use the chivalric conventions when he sees fit. Chivalry gives him a ready-made excuse to keep away hereafter from carriers with staves. Yet why has he not mistaken the staves for lances; why does he so quickly recognize these men for what they really are? The fact is that the action is instigated in this episode by forces outside of Don Quixote. Rocinante smells the mares of the Yanguesans; the carriers in turn beat Rocinante. It is only now that Don Quixote intervenes. The conditions of the fight are established already, and Don Quixote is not the aggressor in the action. It is mainly the adventures which Don Quixote instigates which are the mad ones, the results of the ravings of his disturbed mind. And as is the case with all madmen, the attacks are unpredictable and spasmodic.

* * *

Cervantes' shift from the chaste Marcela and thwarted Chrysostom to Rocinante in his quest of the mares and the violence of the ensuing battle creates striking relief. Cervantes is skillful in varying the tempos and moods of the episodes. The change from Marcela's high-minded rationalizations to the satisfaction of Rocinante's physical needs is indeed a diversion.

Chapter 16

Cervates parodies a situation we find frequently in books of chivalry, the nocturnal visits of knights to their ladies (as in the first chapter of *Amadis of Gaul*), in the attic of the inn where Maritornes comes in search of the carrier. Don Quixote mistakes the Asturian maid for the "daughter of the warden," the carrier beats the maid, the maid beats Sancho, the carrier beats Sancho—all this further confused by darkness. (This is the basis of many such scenes in later novels, such as the bedroom farce involving beau Didapper, Slipslop, and Parson Adams in *Joseph Andrews*.) The riot is interrupted by an officer of the Holy Brotherhood with his wand and box of warrants—ineffectual weapons under the circumstances. Much of Cervantes' satire arises from implied contrasts.

Chapter 17

The balsam of Fierabras, which Don Quixote concocts to cure his wounds, originated in the French geste *Fierabrás* (1170). This was published in Spain in the sixteenth century in translation, but in altered form; it recounts how the Saracen, King Balán and his son, the giant Fierabrás, sacked Rome and stole the sacred relics, "among which were two barrels of the remains of the balsam used to embalm Christ" (RIQ, 107). This balsam could cure the wounds of whoever drank it. In parody of this, Cervantes has Don Quixote mix wine, oil, salt, and rosemary in an oil can. Thus what had been an embalming agent and later a cure for wounds is turned into an emetic. Here Cervantes may be parodying not only the romance, but also the superstitions which gave rise to blind faith in religious panaceas. For the balsam, which does eventually ameliorate Don Quixote's condition, nearly brings death to Sancho.

* * *

Following close on this scene is Sancho's blanket tossing, which he is never to forget. Knight and squire are themselves victims of Don Quixote's mad illusions, often more so than those whom they encounter. Harm, when it is done, tends to rebound.

* * *

In the matter of the payment of the bill, Don Quixote is willing to admit his error in thinking the inn a castle, for knights pay for lodging at neither castles nor inns.

* * *

The officer of the Holy Brotherhood returns, and Don Quixote is ready to accept Sancho's suggestion that the officer is an enchanter, but only after the officer bashes Don Quixote over the head with his lamp. Earlier he has told Sancho that enchanters are invisible. To name the officer an enchanter saves Don Quixote the need for redressing his injury and saves his pride. Again his delusion provides him with an excuse, for one cannot take vengeance on the supernatural. His code, while demanding of him the most rigorous ethic, in practice often provides him with a ready escape from it.

Chapter 18

In this chapter enchanters again provide Don Quixote with an excuse—this time for not coming to Sancho's rescue in the blanket-tossing scene. But Sancho is unwilling to accept such rationalizations. He tells Don Quixote that his tossers were not enchanters, for his assailants had names, and that he is ready to go home. The blanket-tossing episode has been a turning point for Sancho; he is thoroughly disillusioned. To discover the same faults in his master that he himself possesses is too much for him. Without verbalizing his problem, he recognizes that Don Quixote exercises the same "discretion" he himself has determined to practice. Nor will he listen to Don Quixote's words of encouragement. The magic sword Don Quixote promises will, he knows, be no more effective than the balsam was; knights perhaps may benefit from it but not squires.

* * *

This opposition from Sancho appears to churn Don Quixote's brain into another fit of madness. Two flocks of sheep seem to him two great opposing armies. His descriptions of the approach of the sheep burlesque many such passages describing the approach of great armies in the chivalric romances, as well as a passage in the third book of the *Arcadia* of Lope de Vega, one of

Cervantes's contemporaries (RIQ, 112). For a while even Sancho is convinced by the Don's vivid account of the approaching splendor. Too late, Sancho realizes the error. After the battle Don Quixote again invokes his enchanters—one had probably transformed the sheep—and Sancho does not even bother to protest.

Rather, his concern turns to the welfare of his master. The slapstick scene in which Sancho, while inspecting Don Quixote's teeth, receives the regurgitated balsam in his face is worthy of Chaucer's Miller. Sancho is more than ever determined to return home, his faith shattered and his person sullied.

Sancho's comment that Don Quixote would make a better preacher than a knight errant goes to the core of Don Quixote's problem. Don Quixote, like some preachers, tends to emphasize the ideal to the neglect of the real. The remark is double-edged; Cervantes is never flattering when dealing with the clergy.

Chapter 19

In the adventure with the corpse, Sancho's fear of darkness overwhelms him, but Don Quixote is as usual unaware of external reality and takes the priests for knights. This whole episode is an intentional parody of one recounted in the chivalric tale *Palmerin of England,* even to a similarity in the chapter headings. When Don Quixote asks how the knight had been killed, one of the attendants answers that it was by means of a fever. Don Quixote had, however, expected to be answered as Floriano had been in the chivalric tale and to be asked to avenge a great wrong (RIQ, 113-114). Thus Cervantes sharply underlines the difference between the world of fantasy and the everyday world of fact.

Whereas the blanket-tossing has been a crucial experience for Sancho, this episode with the corpse is such an experience for Don Quixote. For the first time he shows some remorse for his action; in fact, his remorse is such that it stirs Sancho to dub him "Knight of the Sad Countenance." He begs pardon of the Bachelor he has wounded; he fears he has incurred excommunication. For an instant the reader believes he will renounce his mad adventure until he remembers a fellow knight—Rodrigo de Vivar—who bore up under excommunication. Both Sancho and Don Quixote have now faced the possibility of renouncing their mission, and both have for the first time turned away from such a renunciation, each in his own fashion—Sancho because of his innate loyalty to his master, Don Quixote because of his innate loyalty to the chivalric ideal.

*   *   *

The secret of Don Quixote's ability to inspire such loyalty in his squire lies in his sharing everything, even the complicity of events, with Sancho. Thus although at this point he realizes he has forgotten his oath to secure Mambrino's helmet, he claims Sancho is also at fault for not reminding him. The adventure is always a *joint* one.

*   *   *

By renaming his master the Knight of the Sad Countenance, Sancho is, of course, following a chivalric tradition. However Cervantes has Don Quixote, in listing other famous titles, omit, perhaps conspicuously, Belíanis' title, "Knight of the Handsome Countenance" and Prince Deocliano's title, "Knight of the Ill-favored Face," Cervantes' obvious source (RIQ, 114). P. E. Russell points out that J. M. Cohen's translation of this title is more in keeping with the Romantic point of view than with that of the Renaissance. *Triste figura* means "a dirty, unprepossessing, ridiculous figure (RUS, 314) and would have had humorous implications for the seventeenth-century reader. Thomas Shelton in 1612 translated the phrase as "Knight of the Ill-favored Face."

Chapter 20

In the episode of the fulling mills, when Sancho ties Rocinante's legs together, Don Quixote does not even get off to see what
has happened to his steed. One suspects again that he is inwardly
glad of an excuse not to explore the noise of the mills. Sancho
often obligingly provides him with such excuses. In fact, when
Sancho suggests that he dismount so he may get some rest, Don
Quixote becomes irate. Knights do not sleep in the midst of
danger, he tells Sancho. But reason, unrecognized by Don Quixote
himself, is creeping into his mind. He cannot yet admit it, though.
His fantasy dies slowly, but every blow Don Quixote receives on
his shoulders is a blow to it as well.

* * *

Sancho's story of the goatherd and his amorous mistress is
indeed a diversion. At the same time one feels Don Quixote's
journey is much like that of the goatherd. One goat at a time is
ferried over the stream just as Don Quixote himself progresses—
haltingly. Furthermore, the story is never ended, for Sancho
claims Don Quixote is not paying attention. Don Quixote, it is
true, is not paying attention to the business of life. Yet when the
fulling hammers are discovered, Don Quixote accepts them for
what they are. His trouble here is that he cannot laugh when
Sancho makes fun of him, and the scene contains one of his rare
outbursts of anger toward Sancho, in which he forbids him to
speak to him in the future. All the same it is possible to see that
one more goat has crossed the stream, for Don Quixote has not
been deceived. Whereas in the episode with the Yanguesans, there
was very little temptation for Don Quixote to be fooled, in this
episode the very conditions—the unidentified sounds, the night,
the immobile Rocinante—would lead the sanest individual into
uncontrollable fantasy. Nevertheless, coming to the fulling ham-

mers in the morning, Don Quixote is dumbfounded and ashamed. Would he not in his earlier adventures have charged the hammers, thinking them giants? Yet madness is an inward state. That which is a frightening image to a so-called sane individual may be an object of small concern to a madman, and vice-versa.

Chapter 21

In the very next episode, however, Don Quixote transforms a barber with a basin on his head into a knight with a golden helmet, that won by Reynaldo of Montalban from the Moorish King Mambrino in Italian chivalric poems (RIQ, 115). We see here how compensation works for Don Quixote and how one episode balances another. "When one door shuts another opens," he remarks. His ego, frustrated by the fulling hammers, is prepared now to make up for this lack of heroism. With the transposition of basin to helmet effected, Don Quixote charges the hapless barber who takes to his heels. It is of interest to note that a barber's basin had an opening for the beard of the customer, an opening which Don Quixote could easily have mistaken for the opening under the visor. (OB, 207)

* * *

Although Sancho identifies with Don Quixote as a madman to some extent, his participation in the chivalric fantasy is in touch with reality in a way that Don Quixote's is not. Thus when Don Quixote tells him of the stages in the ascent of a knight, thereby delineating the stages in the plot common to most chivalric tales, Sancho is ready to receive for himself the *material* benefits of chivalry whereas Don Quixote would share with others its *spiritual* values. His only love is for a Dulcinea he idealizes. Sancho, in contrast, believes that a "leap over the bridge is better than good men's prayers." (169) He is ready to assume the robes of a Duke because he once served as a beadle to a brotherhood. Don Quixote, of course, has also assumed a costume. The difference is that Don Quixote is satisfied with a patched-up suit of armor. Sancho believes that his robes will be covered with *actual* gold and pearls.

Chapter 22

It is possible to see many of the figures in the book as projections in one way or another of Cervantes' own personality. Thus when we meet Gines de Pasamonte in the chapter on the liberation of the galley slaves, we are not surprised to find he has been in prison writing his own life, a clue to what Cervantes may be doing in this book of supposed fiction. In fact, Gines de Pasamonte may be based on a historical figure (Jerónimo de Pasamonte), a soldier who had fought at Lepanto and Navarino and had been held captive in Algiers. He had later written some interesting memoirs—all reminiscent of Cervantes' own life (RIQ, 117). Gines is, of course, the conventional *picaro* of the book, a criminal belonging to the underworld. He tells us that Lazarillo de Tormes, famous hero of a well-known Spanish proto-picaresque tale, will have to look out. Gines is a criminal and a hardened one at that. He instigates the shower of stones which fell the very person who has freed him, and he steals Sancho's ass. He may represent the dark side of Cervantes.

In relation to Don Quixote, Gines points up the fact that deeds done with good intent often end as disastrously as those done with evil intent. Yet Don Quixote's "mistakes" are of a very different nature from Gines' crimes. True, the damage, the loss of property, the pain caused are similar. W. H. Auden puts his finger on the difference when he calls Don Quixote a "holy madman." Although the law of the "Holy" Brotherhood would not recognize the difference, the fact is that Cervantes shows us by means of the comparison of Don Quixote with Gines that one of these men may be saved, the other may not. Good intentions do not pave the way to heaven, but they do not close the gate to it. In fact, they may sometimes lead to a self-knowledge which is a kind of salvation, as in the life of Don Quixote. Evil intentions, on the contrary, always drive an individual to the bowels of the earth, where Gines feels he must hide. It is by such means as these that Cervantes shows the madman as less of a madman than many of the persons he meets. The other characters continually interact with Don Quixote to bring out the hero's nature since no one can be understood without reference to those with whom he comes in contact. Yet as the reader proceeds he recognizes that Don Quixote, like the persons he knows best, will never be fully understood. Cervantes' genius has created a complexity which rivals that of life itself. In other words the book is full of so-called literary 'doubles.'

* * *

Don Quixote gives the order to the sergeant to release the galley slaves, an order likely to instigate political chaos or "a cat with three legs" as the sergeant colorfully puts it. Don Quixote's vow to succor the needy and oppressed is a curious inverse weapon which often accomplishes, as we have seen, the opposite of what it is intended to accomplish. In the episode of the galley slaves, Don Quixote and Sancho are defeated by the very ones they have sought to relieve. The episode illustrates further the results of seeing what one wishes to see in a chain of slaves instead of what the majority of men or at least those in power see. Don Quixote's rationalizations concerning the crimes of these men are as dangerous to organized justice as the crimes themselves. The stones flung by the criminals are perhaps symbolic of their hardened natures. Yet under adversity Don Quixote's nature does not congeal. He is left bruised by the stones, but his main sensation is one of distress at the ingratitude of the slaves. His sense of mission, his love of mankind, his holy madness are not dimmed. Don Quixote's virtues are inner ones, and the pathos of his figure lies in his inability to fit the frame to the picture, to utilize his love for mankind realistically. For as the champion of justice, he

serves the cause of injustice in liberating criminals. The full significance of *quixoticism* is here realized. The episode of the galley
slaves represents a kind of climax, Don Quixote's final attempt
to right a social wrong (PF, 6). And although his sense of mission
is not diminished, his power to act has suffered a severe blow at
the very hands of those he wished to save.

Chapter 23

Don Quixote's rationalizations of his actions are so trans-
parent that both he and Sancho must be aware that they are.
Deciding to flee from the Holy Brotherhood, he makes Sancho
promise never to tell anyone he fled, because the truth is he goes
only to humor Sancho. But what is the truth? In his wakeful
moments Don Quixote sees reality as most men do. Recovering
from the stoning by the galley slaves, he wishes he had followed
Sancho's advice in the first place. Experience is gradually showing
Don Quixote the error of his ways. Yet he is too stubborn, too
dedicated, to give up. We can almost hear him think in this
scene, "Let us retire temporarily, rest in peace for a time and
return reinforced with new vigor. Then let us try once more."
Don Quixote progresses in this fashion, always smarting from
failure, yet always rebounding to make one more try. The episodic
nature of the book fits in with the spasmodic timing of Don
Quixote's illusions.

*　*　*

It is Sancho, though, who gives voice, in a speech reminding
one of Falstaff, to the prudence of the course Don Quixote has
chosen. "It is a wise man's duty to save himself for tomorrow."
Sancho is continually bringing to the surface the thoughts that
people Don Quixote's unconscious. This is only one aspect of
the complex relation between master and squire, a relationship

in which roles are continually being exchanged, shared, or put into new perspective. In this way Cervantes avoided oversimplifying the treatment of character, unlike many of his contemporaries or the authors of books of chivalry.

The comparison between the comic figures of Falstaff and of Sancho is of some interest, too. They differ chiefly because of the different contexts in which they appear. Yet both are products of the Renaissance, presenting in one sense the Rabelaisian element of the era. Both love good food, drink, and wenches. Yet despite his interaction with Henry V, Falstaff stands relatively alone; Sancho is one of a pair. Here we can see how a character is molded by his particular constellation. Sancho's main function is to act as a foil to Don Quixote. Falstaff, on the contrary, ends by stealing an entire play. There is no one else in *Henry IV* of comparable "stature." Sancho's speech on discretion can be seen as a vocalizing of the thought of his otherworld counterpart. Falstaff's "better part of valour" speech proposes a philosophy which represents Falstaff alone. The functions, then, of the two characters are what differentiate them; their "discretion" in the face of danger is similar. The intricacy of the relationship between Sancho and his master is what forms one of the challenges of this book.

Walter Kaiser points out in his chapter on *Don Quixote* in *Praisers of Folly* that unlike Falstaff, Sancho is not rejected by the world. Rather he triumphs in the end, thus reversing the usual treatment of folly. Furthermore, the fact that the master is mad and the squire foolish results in the lack of a fixed point, in a relativistic uncertainty or an ambiguity about the nature of wisdom and folly. (This is, of course, the main issue of Erasmus' *Moriae encomium.*) The barber, the priest, and others infected by the contagion of chivalry seem even more foolish, then, when it is seen that they have been the dupes of fools (K, 281-288).

Chapter 24

As we have noted, the digressions always form patterns with the main theme. Cardenio's madness and Don Quixote's provide an interesting contrast. Both come in fits and both are provoked by opposition. But Don Quixote's madness is madness with a purpose. Cardenio's madness is undirected and meaningless. It is defensive madness; Don Quixote's is offensive in the sense of being missionary. Cardenio is defending his own honor at being called a liar and a scoundrel. Don Quixote, in contrast, is unmindful of personal honor when his lady and the order of knighthood are at stake. His entire crusade is directed toward unselfish aims, heedlesss of personal loss. Once again this madman is shown to be more sane than those he meets, even jilted Cardenio. The whole world has jilted Don Quixote, and yet it is this world he wishes to save. Is not love always sheer madness? And is it not Don Quixote alone who has really understood books of chivalry, and the world at large which has accepted and understood only the superficial aspects of these books? Don Quixote then acts out the chivalric role, an acting out which mocks superficially the understanding of the mass of readers of *Amadis of Gaul*. But at the same time the pasteboard vizor and barber's basin suffice for him because he sees beyond these outward insignia, whereas for the average man the badge (the insignia) makes the man. It is not the virtues of chivalry which Cervantes deplores; it was not for them that books of chivalry were banned in some areas at the time. It is rather the temptation, encouraged by these books, to place the emphasis on trivialities, to glorify physical prowess and worldly wealth at the expense of the spirit, a temptation counteracted by Cervantes and the Don. And so in a very real sense the book is, as the author states in his prologue, "an invective against books of chivalry," although it is at the same time the greatest chivalric romance ever written. Don Quixote's spirituality is rugged and angular by comparison with the sugar-coated spirituality of, for example, Malory's Percival. Even Sancho's worldliness is always subordinate to his ultimate loyalty to and love of his master. So Don Quixote and Sancho ride through the world serving as grotesque reminders to mankind of its own faults, acting as mirrors for those who would see them as such. Should we not all stop to take stock of the pasteboard vizors and the barbers' basins with which our own houses are filled—the masks which shield and separate us from our fellow men?

Chapter 25

Chapter 25, entitled "The Knight's Penitence," provides further illumination on the subject of madness which preoccupies Cervantes here as it did Shakespeare in *King Lear,* particularly in the scene (Act III, scene 6) showing the madmen, Lear, the Fool, and Edgar (as poor Tom). The contrast between the mad Cardenio and Don Quixote has already been made. Now Don Quixote, the so-called "madman," determines to go mad. Furthermore, he declares he will go mad for no reason at all. This is to be a madness not of deeds, but of tears and grief. Don Quixote is doubling his complicity in the chivalric fiction when he imitates the penance of Amadis of Gaul and the demented fury of Orlando, spurned by his love. He presumes thereby that he has not been mad up to this point, but he also unconsciously comments upon himself by showing us that madness is something that can be assumed as he has assumed the role of knight. Don Quixote's assumption of a mad role is superficially comparable to Edgar's assumption of madness as a disguise or the Fool's employment of madness in his profession (depending on one's reading of the Fool). The involuntary madness which Don Quixote suffers is sharply contrasted with the madness he has voluntarily assumed when he turns his attention here momentarily to Mambrino's helmet. Sancho tells Don Quixote he is "cracked in the brain" to see a helmet in a barber's basin. Don Quixote, aware only unconsciously of this level of his madness, reverts to enchanters to explain to Sancho his view of the basin. But is it not true that the value and function of an object depend on our point of view toward it? Is it, then, madness to say that helmet is basin or basin, helmet? On the contrary, the charm of Don Quixote's knight errantry seems to be that through it a knight may remake the world in his own image. It is when he takes off his clothes in this scene, becomes naked, that he becomes really mad. Don Quixote's fiction of knighthood, then, his need for the symbolic helmet as part of his mission, seems essentially more meaningful than the consciously assumed role of spurned lover. He is taking on the relatively aimless pursuit of Cardenio in the preceding episode. Lear's involuntary madness is an aimless madness, yet Don Quixote's involuntary madness has a meaning. It is when he pretends madness, imitates Amadis who was presumably performing sane acts in terms of chivalry, that Don Quixote becomes insane. The terrifying reflection on Don Quixote's involuntary madness is that it is undirected, holy though the intentions may be. Thus his values are never applied in the real world except by misdirection or by chance. The madness Don Quixote shows *for no reason,* however, such as the penance he performs for Dulcinea, is even worse. I think Cervantes is saying here that play-acting in life for the sake of play-acting does not work, is not authentic. Faith or belief in one's role and in a purpose or end is a basic need if a man is to be an effective agent. And even if one possesses this faith, whether mad or sane, one is still not certain of producing good results.

To return to Shakespeare, we see that Edgar feigns madness for a purpose; the Fool may have been mad, but has regained his sanity sufficiently to direct his madness to an end. Of the three madmen in *Lear,* Edgar is the most purposeful, Lear the least. The Fool is like Don Quixote; in one way his profession is dependent on his madness. But the Fool is able to direct his words and actions in his attempt to help his master; Don Quixote assumes the mission of protecting the whole world, but he cannot master himself. The entire question of insanity was a subject of much importance in Renaissance literature. Wayward spirits were no longer the sole concern of the church and of exorcising priests.

Don Quixote is satisfied to "imagine and believe" (210) that Aldonza Lorenzo is lovely, but this is the only point in the novel where he admits Dulcinea is a peasant girl. (Riquer points out that this indicates a momentary sanity [RIQ, 120].) Yet, although he knows her to be a farm girl, he tells Sancho his acts of penance "are not in jest, but very much in earnest" (207). At the same time, he states that his purpose is merely to imitate Amadis even though he has been spurned by no maiden (203).

His real madness is, of course, a holy madness, one devoted to an ideal Dulcinea, which is contrasted in this chapter to madness for the sake of madness. Play-acting for its own sake is too often, as Cervantes saw, a part of too many lives in this world. Cervantes also parodies the fact that writers of books of chivalry tended to imitate other writers of such books simply for the sake of imitation and not for any real reason. Their characterizations often lacked, therefore, any true motivation.

*   *   *

The irony in Sancho's description of Aldonza Lorenzo should not be overlooked. Don Quixote could not have failed to pick a Dulcinea who was poles apart from his image of her. "She will know how to keep her chin out of the mud," Sancho tells us, and "What a pair of lungs" (209).

The irony, of course, stems from the implied contrast between Sancho's description of Dulcinea and the descriptions of lovely ladies in the chivalric romances. Likewise the letter Don Quixote writes to Dulcinea is an exact parody of letters knights and ladies write in books of chivalry. For example, Don Quixote's letter opens as does a letter from Oriana to Amadis of Gaul, "I am the maid whose heart was wounded by a sword point" (RIQ, 121). Readers in the seventeenth century were familiar with books of chivalry, and they must have understood Cervantes' parodic purposes. Furthermore, this particular letter serves as a double parody, for in the next chapter when Sancho tries to repeat to the priest and barber, he distorts it, substituting, "Sublime and suppressed lady," for "Sovereign and sublime lady" and calling Dulcinea thankless and ungrateful.

Chapter 26

After Sancho leaves on his mission to Dulcinea, Don Quixote decides on a milder course of penance. That is, Don Quixote at first felt that he had to threaten violent action to convince Sancho that his intentions were firm, but he then rationalized prudence in his actions. His conscious reasoning is irrational, and more and more often he is trying to find means and reasons to shy away from direct confrontation of his fantasy. It exists more easily if it is not continually tested. More and more often, too, we are reminded that Don Quixote's interpretation of his role is changing. The pathos of his character grows as he slowly learns that the most that ever will be said of him is that he "attempted" great things, that his intentions were good ones. And the pathos deepens because even his intentions are questioned by most men he meets.

Chapter 27

Cervantes continually uses disguises, which were so popular with Shakespeare and other Elizabethans, for mistaken identity was then a favorite form of comedy. The Renaissance writer tells us in essence, not that a change of clothes will remake the man, but rather that the disguise symbolizes what from time to time we all do when we adopt a role—for good or for ill. Thus the priest, disguised as "errant damsel" (with heavy irony on Cervantes' part), and the barber as his squire with an ox-tail beard play parts assigned them by the priest which are later reversed when the priest decides his clothes are unfitted for a member of the clergy.

Two kinds of play-acting may again be compared—that which is conscious and that which is unconscious. Perhaps the priest's role of "damsel errant" comes too close to the suppressed truth for comfort and to exchange skirts for the ox-tail beard is to assume a real disguise. For it may be noted that he leaves his cassock as security for the landlady's dress and that his nightcap, his black taffeta garters, his hat, and his cloak serve as part of his female disguise. Later he states that it is indecent for churchmen to appear in such garb; he may be saying that priests should not dress as priests. Again, perhaps the conscious role is for the moment too close to the real and suppressed role. At the same time, the costume of priesthood must have offered to such a person considerable conscious or unconscious fulfillment. Cervantes' humanism is not without its subtleties.

* * *

It is of some interest that in 1613 a lost comedy, probably by Shakespeare and Fletcher, *The History of Cardenio* that deals with the love affairs of Cardenio and Lucinda, and Ferdinand and Dorothea, was acted in London before the king. The first part of *Don Quixote,* translated by Thomas Shelton, had appeared in England in 1612. In light of this, scholars might profitably consider the possible influence of *Don Quixote* on Shakespeare's last plays.

* * *

The romance element which unfolds in the digressions concerning Cardenio, Lucinda, Don Ferdinand, and Dorothea provides significant contrasts with the Gothic element of the main plot. While Don Quixote is pretending madness for his Dulcinea and imitating Amadis of Gaul in his devotion to his loved one,

Cardenio is in reality mad for his Lucinda (almost an anagram for Dulcinea). His is not ideal madness, no medieval chivalric mania. Without Lucinda he does not desire health. Both in their madness compose poetry in the courtly tradition and on the subject of their grief. But Don Quixote has experienced no treachery. No Don Ferdinand has cheated him and no Lucinda supposedly deceived him. Why then does the Knight do penance at all? Is the whole performance only an empty imitation of Amadis of Gaul? The contrast with Cardenio brings out, on the contrary, the mock-Christ or Gothic element in Don Quixote. Don Quixote does penance not for Lucinda, but for the human race which mocks and cheats him. A Don Ferdinand may not have deceived him, but many others have and will. His penance is a symbolic penance; the chivalric waste lands of the Percivals and the Don Quixotes are steps on the path to the cross. Cardenio's grief, on the other hand, does not reach beyond itself, and he talks only of that grief and of threats of self-destruction. Thus two kinds of self-destruction are compared: Don Quixote desires to erase pride, the cognizance of the *I,* so that his mission may be a single-minded one. Cardenio, in contrast, would do away with his body.

The digressions serve as foils and parallels to the main plot and highlight the Gothic multi-angularity of the novel's hero. His spirituality stands above and beyond the simple and naïve physical existence of the young lovers. Cervantes also allows a note of haunting nostalgia for the idyllic life to creep in, especially in the figures of Clara and her mule boy, in contrast to the more difficult spiritual life. Yet above all of them towers the figure of the hero on his angular mount followed by his faithful squire astride his ass.

Chapter 28

Superficial though most of the characters in the digressions
appear to be, Dorothea is the one figure of some depth. Her
strength of mind, her understanding of others' problems, and her
pursuit of Don Ferdinand make her a worthy counterpart for the
hero, Don Quixote. Dorothea's purpose in leaving home has not
been to pursue a course of senseless grieving in the mountains,
but to confront her lover with what he has done. When she
cannot find him and is assaulted by her own servant (whom she
forces over a precipice), she takes a herding job disguised in
shepherd's clothes. It is not until her employer discovers her
sex and is himself about to assault her that she determines to take
to the mountains where she can indulge in sighs and tears. All
of her acts, as well as her willingness and ingenuity in assuming
the role of Princess Micomicona, make us respect her more than
we do the other figures in the digressions. Cervantes usually refers to her as "sensible." She is a capably-drawn woman—much
more real than her lover Don Ferdinand, who plays the stage
villain until his sudden reformation. Especially fine is Cervantes'
description of Dorothea's beauty—her feet in the brook were like
"two pieces of pure crystal" (237). Riquer notes that Dorothea
may be drawn from a life model (RIQ, 281). Lucinda and Clara,
in contrast, are conventional fictional figures for furthering the
plot.

If this is a book about the destroying of illusions which all
of us face continually, then, Dorothea's lack of illusions contrasts
pleasantly with the illusions which most of the other characters
entertain. Don Quixote's own illusions are by no means practical.
To the contrary, Dorothea knows that her lover is a scoundrel, but
for the sake of their public honor, a most practical consideration,
she undertakes her dangerous journey. She has no illusions about
her man, about herself, or about others. Her single consideration

is a niche in her society where she may fit with some comfort. To this end, which is the end Don Quixote longs to attain at the conclusion of the book, she sacrifices first her purity and then appearances. Without an author sympathetic to her plight, however, Dorothea could hardly have won at her game. Still, she does not envision a rosy future for herself; in the repentance scene when all the company, even Don Ferdinand, are close to tears, Dorothea is able to speak to him "briefly and sensibly" about her recent adventures. Fictional device though it may be, Don Ferdinand's sudden turn of heart awaits the testing of time, and Dorothea knows it.

Chapter 29

The status of the black man in these times is clear. Sancho is disturbed at the idea that his subjects may be black. But he consoles himself with the scheme of selling them as slaves and buying a title with his earnings.

* * *

Cervantes' subtle ironies concerning priests continue throughout the book. He points out the village priest's love of talk rather than action again and again—as when the priest insists on instructing Dorothea how to play the role of Princess Micomicona, for which she needs no tutoring, the role in which he had originally cast himself. Yet during the confrontation of Dorothea and Don Quixote the priest decides his own presence is not necessary.

* * *

Further irony is evident in Don Quixote's discovery of the priest's ability to refix beards, explained to Don Quixote as a charm. In reality, the priest has simply stuck Master Nicholas' beard back on, but the episode may be a sarcastic commentary on the priest as a dispenser of the holy mysteries.

* * *

A final topical reference in this chapter concerns the Holy Brotherhood, which according to the priest was undisturbed for years before Don Quixote freed the galley slaves. Perhaps it was time, the reader concludes, that someone stirred them up. Yet Don Quixote's stirrings are always unfortunately misdirected. We see the priest cleverly use his knowledge of the episode to shame Don Quixote. According to the priest, these same galley slaves Don Quixote set free robbed him and the barber, Master Nicholas. Don Quixote has not the courage to confess to his own deed. Is he not gradually, in Cervantes' own words, "changing color?"

Chapter 30

The grouping of episodes in the chapters shows Cervantes' genius for storytelling. From Dorothea's invention of her role as Princess Micomicona in this chapter, he moves to Don Quixote's attack on Sancho for his disparaging words about Dulcinea, and then to Sancho's recovery of his ass. The whole chapter is tied together at the end by the commentary of Cardenio and the Priest. A final paragraph on Sancho's visit to Dulcinea leads smoothly into the next chapter. In Chapter 30 events fluctuate between the imaginary and the real as they do throughout the entire book and in the mind of the hero. Dorothea's ingenious tale is, of course, sheer fantasy, yet fantasy invented for a worthwhile purpose. This world of imagination is suddenly confronted with the real world when Don Quixote knocks down Sancho. He does so because Sancho will not and cannot accept an ideal and imaginary Dulcinea, especially when he sees that she conflicts with his promised governorship, which is so far a highly imaginary one for Sancho. Sancho's blows are, however, made less painful by the easy recovery of Dapple from a fearful Gines de Pasamonte, showing perhaps that desires are less dangerous if they can be realized at least partially and that imagination may be put to good use.

* * *

Cardenio's comment that a man would have difficulty inventing such a character as Don Quixote in fiction really is Cervantes' commentary on his own genius. Will it work? Like all writers he is beset by doubts about it, and so he stops to query. Don Quixotes do exist; the most difficult task of the writer is to penetrate and capture them. Preposterous characters abound in fiction, yet Cervantes wants more than this. He wants to draw a man who is not totally irrational, but who is, as the priest says, rational in every respect except for chivalry. Cervantes himself puts to good use his powers of fantasy as Dorothea had used her fantasy to invent the story of the princess. Don Quixote, dreaming of chivalry, infecting Sancho with dreams of power and wealth, inflicting damages and committing errors across the face of Spain, indulges in fantasy, but with undesirable results. In this chapter, Cervantes succeeded in contrasting not only the real and the imaginary but the constructive and destructive possibilities of fantasy. The complexity and subtlety of his writing is well demonstrated here. Balances, counterbalances, appositions, and parallels everywhere abound. No episode or group of episodes exist without devious paths.

* * *

It is of interest to compare Dorothea's chivalric fantasies with those of Don Quixote. Her purpose is different from Quixote's and yet similar. Like him she desires to assist those in distress and like him she assumes a role. However, she is aware that she uses a *deception* in order to achieve her purpose. Don Quixote does not admit that the chivalric life is a deception. Furthermore, there is in her story a humorous undercurrent whereby she consciously parodies the cihvalric mode. Don Quixote, as has been noted, is never able to laugh at his own fantasies, even after the night spent beside the fulling mill. Don Quixote fits reality into his fiction, whereas Dorothea creates a fiction without deforming reality (RIQ, 123). The culminating irony of this contrast is, of course, that Don Quixote, rather than rescuing "maidens in distress," becomes in this chapter a knight in distress who is rescued by a maiden.

Chapter 31

Sancho recognized the nature of his master's madness after Don Quixote admitted, in Chapter 25, Aldonza's parentage. He felt, as a result, that he had the license to invent his *own* fictions about Dulcinea, which he does for the first time on his supposed return from El Toboso. But Don Quixote does not forsake his image of Dulcinea even in the face of Sancho's account of his visit to her. Dulcinea winnowing red wheat, running with sweat, and tearing up Don Quixote's letter is a Dulcinea Don Quixote does not admit to despite Sancho's supposed testimony. Because Don Quixote desires to believe in his ideal mistress, he is able to overlook even the evidence of his senses. And whenever he can no longer fail to hear the voice of reality, he invents an enchanter, for instance, to speed Sancho to El Toboso and back (90 miles) in three days. Cervantes thereby defines the meaning of the word *faith*.

Sancho is not deluded. He knows the truth, but in his confusion over maintaining his deceit he makes a bad slip and tells Don Quixote that Dulcinea desires that her knight return home— forgetting completely his kingdom awaiting him in the land of Micomicon. Because he is not deluded about reality, Sancho also can never be thoroughly convinced of the knight's genuineness. Unlike Don Quixote he has read no books of chivalry, indeed no books at all. His inspiration must come to him then second-hand, and one sees again and again that Sancho is torn between returning home and achieving the governorship Don Quixote has promised him. This lack of single-minded purpose is partly what lends the comic element to the Sancho figure. He has a wavering foot in two camps as even his errors of speech indicate. Yet Sancho rises above his dilemma in that his love for his master transcends the issue between the Quixadas and the Quixotes of this world. (Andrew, whom we meet for a second time, is, unlike Sancho, by now completely devoid of faith. Beaten by his master, stripped of his wages, he sees that knight errantry avails nothing. "God blast you and every knight errant" (276) are his parting words to Don Quixote.)

By means of these episodes, Cervantes indicates that Don Quixote is not completely to be despised, especially in terms of his *real* contemporaries. His single-minded devotion to his ideal stands up rather well against Sancho's frantic desire for power as governor (a power he doubtless lacks at home) and his conflicting need on occasion to run home to the protection of Juana-Teresa. And as for Andrew, one does not doubt that his devotion to his job was anything but single-minded and that if Don Quixote had not happened along to spur the farmer employer, something else would have fired his anger. As in the case of the galley slaves, Andrew was doubtless not being chastised without some justification. It is worth noting that none of the company save Sancho will vouchsafe Andrew a piece of bread.

Still we cannot forget that Cervantes uses Andrew's second appearance as yet another reminder that Don Quixote's purposes, noble though they may be, never are accomplished. Hospitalization of a fellow man and permanent injury to him are, after all, pretty high prices to pay for one's ideals, and Don Quixote is right in his abashment at Andrew's story. It is simply one more of the jolts which are to bring Don Quixote finally back to his senses. However, he awakens to his real nobility too late, which only completes the tragic definition of his story. But for the reader, enlightenment comes before the adventures are completed, and in this scene he may view the horror in his own false idealisms as Cervantes holds up the mirror of his hero's life.

Chapter 32

The host at the inn to which the travelers return is also an avid reader of books of chivalry. His only reason for not turning knight is that it is no longer the fashion. But his belief in the truth of these books is as profound as Don Quixote's, and when the priest suggests that some books of chivalry are pure fiction the innkeeper nearly goes out of his mind with anger. The more outrageous and unbelievable a tale, the greater is the innkeeper's delight. In his own words the books make him "go mad with pleasure" (280). The priests's criterion in judging these books is how truthful he thinks they are. Some which tell true-life histories he deems harmless. But to the innkeeper the real adventures are tame beside the imaginary ones he prefers, such as the one in which Felixmarte of Hyrcania cuts five giants in half with one backstroke.

It is easy to see why books of chivalry had been banned in some areas (*e.g.,* the West Indies) at the time and why the church in all countries tended to frown on them. They represent the world of illusion, and illusions are outside the control of the church and state. Miracle and mystery may be condoned only as instruments of the church. Let loose they lead to dangerous flights of fancy which threaten established authority. The burning of books such as that which occurred at the beginning of *Don Quixote,* is, however, an ineffectual way of destroying their content, especially if they have already infested the minds of men. Man's need for illusions outside and beyond his everyday reality is recognized by both church and state, and it is a need both attempt to channel and to fulfill—the church with its holy mysteries and the state with its "holidays" or its royalty.

Because illusions, especially those which lead in the direction of anarchy, are strongly suppressed in any state, it is the fate of the Don Quixotes to be forced to live without the very elements which keep them alive. The innkeeper, however, stands more in awe of public opinion than Don Quixote. As a married man he must earn a living and to take up chivalry as a vocation just would not do; it was not "the fashion." Don Quixote is more a free agent than the innkeeper.

Mia I. Gerhardt points out that Cervantes was interested in portraying different kinds of readers (GER, 17-24). Thus we have Don Diego, the naïve humanist; Don Lorenzo, the intelligent humanist; the priest and the canon, readers of the cloth; shepherds in the pastoral tradition, who live literature as a game; and the host at the inn, who is dependent on others to read to him. Don Quixote is perhaps closest to the illiterate host, for both identify completely with the characters. As we have said, the only difference is that the host has enough sense to remain *passively* involved. By contrasting the various reasons people read books, Cervantes is able to approach from still another angle the basic problem of truth and illusion. For the many different kinds of readers show us that, because the truth is always a matter of perspective, who is to decide whether the helmet is of gold or merely a barber's basin? All these readers abandon themselves, although in different ways, to the dream of Don Quixote. Even the Canon, who disapproves of books of chivalry, has tried to write one himself. The problem of the reality of literature, then, and the ambiguous play of truth and lie is brought out through the reactions of various readers. For how is man able to judge except through his own perspective?

Still perhaps the most astonishing miracle of the whole book is that the Holy Brotherhood never does quite catch up with Don Quixote. He walks in a world of his own making, immune to the laws which govern his fellow man, leaving a trail of dead sheep and freed prisoners. Perhaps it is simply a stroke of luck for Don Quixote, or perhaps Cervantes tries to tell us that Don Quixote and his mad fantasies appeal even to the very people he injures and that he acts as a projection for them so that innkeepers do not have to leave their inns and guards do not have to leave their prisoners to engage in the chivalric adventure. Those people who act out our own impossible whimsies for us save us from ourselves as Christ saved the world from itself by assuming the cross. It is here that the true depth of Auden's term "holy madman" for Don Quixote may be discovered. The innkeeper with his interest in chivalric lore throws Don Quixote into a new light, and all the other characters comment upon or place in perspective the complex nature of the hero, even Maritornes, at the beginning of the chapter, who sees in books of chivalry simply the love scenes. The books themselves, as the innkeeper wisely observes, cannot be to blame. Books are only mirrors and can reflect only what we ourselves give them to reflect.

Chapter 33

"The Tale of Foolish Curiosity," the plot of which was derived from Canto 43 of Ariosto's *Orlando Furioso,* deals with a husband without the sense to leave well enough alone. Like Don Quixote, Anselmo seeks an ideal but seeks it in the wrong way—by attempting to make his wife "prove" her virtue. As Don Quixote dons armor and mounts nag, so Anselmo arranges the props for his stage production. He sets up a false situation to satisfy his ego which he himself admits is sick. Lothario's conduct, on the contrary, may be compared to Sancho's. Aware of his friend's poor judgment, Lothario launches into a long and ineffective sermon on the ill-advised plan to seduce Camilla. Yet in the end he succumbs to the plea of his friend and blindly follows the leader, as Sancho follows Don Quixote. And as with Sancho—as the mission continues his own worst interests begin to be served. Sancho's desire for power is whetted, whereas Lothario's lust is stirred by the continual proximity of Camilla.

Here then are two further figures who serve to show up the triviality of the average man in comparison to the significance of the hero. Anselmo is a man grappling with the ghost of infidelity; Don Quixote grapples with Abraham's angel. Only the sense of mission, of purpose, of otherness saves Don Quixote in the end. That he cares for his fellow man is undeniable; Anselmo, on the contrary, cares only for his own interests.

Chapter 34

The tragedy arising from Anselmo's madness deepens as the tale unfolds, and the play-acting becomes even more apparent as Anselmo becomes more willing to be duped. Cervantes employs the romance device of hiding an eavesdropper behind the tapestries, who, in this case, hears Camilla assert her virtue by means of apparent attempted suicide. As a result he receives Lothario again into his home. The complications caused by Leonela (little lion) and her lover remind one of a Shakespearean comedy. Actually the influence of the romance, a popular contemporary form noted for its artificiality, is clearly evident in the digression. Furthermore, the gulled husband was a favorite subject of Renaissance humor. Such brazen unfaithfulness, however, is difficult to accept in the light of the fact that Camilla and Lothario had been sterling characters beforehand, and Anselmo's belief in his wife is difficult to accept in the light of the suspicions he held when there were no grounds for them. Still, these sudden shifts must be seen simply as poetic license. Furthermore, the husband most certain of his wife's honor will be the husband most difficult to convince of her dishonor, and it is clear that Anselmo never would have hatched his plan at all had he envisioned that either Camilla or Lothario would succumb. Rather it is an amusement, a divertissement, to put friend and wife thus to the test. Anselmo is using them for his own satisfactions and pretexts—as if they were things, not people.

Don Quixote, on the contrary, often imagines things to be people, but he never turns people into things. The self-centered man, the egotist, must, however, be surrounded by objects, for people provide a friction and interaction which he is unprepared to meet since it interrupts his view of himself. It is of some interest that Don Quixote himself is not present while this tale is being read, almost as if Cervantes were saying that his hero does not need the lesson embodied therein. For the others, however, this digression supplies a warning against a frivolous self-love. In comparison with the Don, Anselmo appears to be the madder.

Chapter 35

Almost as if to prove his point, Cervantes inserts into the middle of the tale the encounter of Don Quixote with the wineskins. Even in his sleep upstairs Don Quixote is busy repairing wrongs and attacking giants—thinking the wineskins to be the Princess Micomicona's great enemy. For material reasons entirely Sancho is willing to believe the giant has been slain. Meanwhile the innkeeper laments his lost wine.

The point of all this is clear. Even in his sleep Don Quixote is more successful than Anselmo in his waking hours: Anselmo, thinking to prove his wife's virtue, has destroyed his marriage, and Don Quixote, thinking that he attacks evil, has destroyed another's property. Friends come to his aid, pay for the damage, gently propel him toward home. Loved because in his intentions he is the least frivolous of men, Don Quixote survives the results of his errors, and when the reader stops to consider, he finds it difficult to judge which enterprises in this life are real and which illusory, the social interplay of the Anselmos, the spiritual exercises of the priest, the military exploits of the knight—*which* are simply means of passing time?

Don Quixote later discusses the relative merits of arms and of letters. He makes it clear, as do these episodes, that the knight, unlike the scholar, risks his life, becomes involved with others and for others to the point of sacrificing his own being. There is no more that a man can do, and it is with this dedication that Don Quixote conducts himself. If such sacrifice also is illusion, then the whole humanistic system of which Cervantes is a product collapses. With the Renaissance, Christ does come to this earth, and His crucifixion becomes the fate of the Renaissance hero, its Don Quixotes and its Cids. Shakespeare's tragic heroes all recog-

nize their self-centeredness, but too late. Don Quixote, in con-
trast, shows what happens when love is present but misdirected.
Herein lies the crux of the difference between the madness of Don
Quixote and of Lear. Lear suffers because he cannot love others;
Don Quixote suffers, although he loves others, because he cannot
transform that love into meaningful deeds. Shakespeare's trage-
dies are almost all concerned with the interior problem of pride;
Don Quixote's natural humility is to the contrary tragically wasted.

Chapter 36

   Don Ferdinand's change of heart is one of the seemingly most
artificial aspects of the book. Still, such changes were customary
in contemporary romances, and a husband, no matter what his
character had been, is considered to be better than no husband
at all. As has already been noted, Dorothea's eyes are open to her
future. "I am still your wife, whether you like it or not" (328)
she tells Don Ferdinand. The personal wishes of both are meaningless in the face of the demands of the society of which they are
part. The European marriage often has been a social arrangement
rather than an emotional fulfillment. With all her good sense,
Dorothea is able to bring reason to bear on her problem. She
catches her man thereby. But for Cervantes to make Don Ferdinand almost burst into tears with "love and repentance" (331)
seems to be obvious fictional tampering. Better that he also recognize that his marriage is a social obligation. Perhaps, however,
a declaration of love under the circumstances was the most tactful
move Don Ferdinand could have made, a move calculated to set
the tone of the marriage which at least to the world must seem
like a marriage. Dorothea herself in her speeches has already accepted such an arrangement. She tells Don Ferdinand she loves
him but is aware of her lack of noble status. Her chief concern
in his leaving her is the gossip it will cause (328) and the shame
to her parents in their old age. It seems, then, that behind the

apparent lack of realism in this scene there lies a deeper realism, the acceptance by two young people of the social norm—an acceptance Don Quixote makes or desires too late. Dorothea is thoroughly practical and accepts the demands of her society—quite the opposite from the hero—Don Quixote. We see her here as a foil for him. And it is she who saves the honor of Don Ferdinand, for which he gives thanks to heaven. The hero, on the contrary, is able to save no one. He awakes only after the reconciliations have been accomplished.

Chapter 37

Some insight into the feelings of Moor and Christian for one another in Renaissance Spain is possible when we meet the captive and his Moorish lady, Zoraida. Even the "sensible" Dorothea hopes the veiled lady is not a Moor. Zoraida's eagerness to be baptized is all that saves her in the eyes of the assembled company. She even disclaims her own name in favor of Maria. Prejudice in all centuries takes the same form and arises from the same causes. Any minority faction which threatens in any way the established order and custom is likely to suffer prejudice. Dorothea's feelings seem to be taken for granted by Cervantes. He indicates in no way that her response should have been different. For those who would disclaim the fact of progress, a glance at this scene might be fruitful. An unanalytical approach to social phenomena characterized medieval and early Renaissance Europe. Today our attitudes are under constant probing. Awareness of problems can only lead to examined attitudes.

Chapter 38

Don Quixote's defense of arms in this chapter must be considered in the light of the late medieval and Renaissance tradition which viewed the practice of arms as a means of acquiring virtues. It was closely connected, as Maravall shows, with the possibility that man could be reformed, and even with the idea of Empire (MAR, 16). It assumed that man was perfectible and that true nobility was not hereditary but might be achieved. The nobility of the *honrado,* Maravall states (MAR, 124), was a personal and enduring nobility bearing with it public honor and privileges. This new sense of "chivalry" was rooted in the thought of the period, and in this respect *Don Quixote* differs from the chivalric romance. Don Quixote's idealisms spring in part from his belief in the "humanism of arms," and it is because arms may be used for worthwhile purposes that Cervantes' satire of the amusements of "chivalry" is so sharp.

* * *

Don Quixote's discourse on arms and letters (a typical Renaissance topic particularly appropriate for Cervantes as a man both of arms and letters) is a curious inverse of his experience. Don Quixote's triumphs are those of the spirit, those of intention; his failures are all in the world of arms. Yet in his discourse he defends arms against letters on the grounds that peace is the highest aim a man can have and that the soldier's life is harder and less rewarding than that of the man of letters. Don Quixote himself has rarely succeeded in establishing peace, but that his life is full of hardship is undeniable. Does the extent of the hardship qualify one profession as superior to another? He makes here a plea for the honor which comes from self-sacrifice. The spirit which informs Don Quixote is not one which seeks out the easiest way. Hardship and suffering are to be prized as leading to salvation. So again we do not admire him for his soldierly deeds but for what he intended to be and to become in embracing his militant life. The very fact that he does discourse on theoretical matters and propose a set of values shows him to be a man engaged in labors of the spirit. After all, he is middle-aged, his horse is old, his helmet shattered. Thus as he talks to his admiring listeners, we see that his very existence belies what he is saying and that spirit after all does triumph over matter, letters over arms. A hint of this recognition may lie in Don Quixote's own unconscious, for he concludes his discourse with a diatribe against artillery—which he claims has removed the honor from the profession of war. A coward who flees from the report of his own gun may fire a musket and kill a man. Honor in war, then, is at the mercy of the art of weaponry; honor in letters is in no way linked to the temporal world. Don Quixote blames the age he lives in, but he did not live to face, lance poised in hand, an exploding atomic bomb.

The attitude of the listeners to Don Quixote's discourse shows well the Renaissance attitude toward *madness*. The company marvels at the intelligence and understanding Don Quixote shows, yet pities him for his mania concerning chivalry. To understand why Don Quixote has not long since been confined behind bars, it is necessary to understand the tolerance with which the Renaissance viewed aberrations of the mind. They were not so much diseases as abnormal characteristics. Don Quixote is not considered sick; he is considered mad, at least on one subject. True, Don Quixote is gently propelled toward home and rest by friends, nevertheless, much time has passed without his once having been confronted by the authorities. Apparently most of the people he has met have considered his antics as relatively harmless. Only the freeing of the galley slaves seems to have set off an official reaction. Madness was regarded as simply a different way of adjusting, one not taken by the normal man. Unless it seriously interfered with other peoples' lives, it was more or less tolerated and sometimes provided a source of entertainment. Our modern judgment of madness as a disease may be simply a moral judgment, not a medical one. Medieval madhouses were never staffed by doctors, (see Thomas S. Szasz *The Ethic of Psycho-*

analysis, N.Y. 1965). The King's fool was a familiar figure in medieval courts. It was the eighteenth century with its fear of disorder and the nineteenth with its moral climate that propelled madness toward its present category of "mental illness."

Chapter 39

The captive's tale which Cervantes relates in Chapters 39, 40, and 41 provided him with the opportunity to insert an eyewitness account of battles he himself had taken part in, especially the famous battle of Lepanto—the last important stand made by the Turks against European Christianity, and a battle in which Cervantes himself was wounded and taken captive. Much has been written to show that Cervantes was not simply a man of letters. The profession of arms was for him as for his hero a noble one, and he fought bravely and well. Of all the chapters in the book, Chapter 39 alone refers in some detail to topical affairs of Cervantes' time. Still, the main issue of *Don Quixote* is an issue of letters versus arms, and the captive may have spoken truly when he suggested that his youngest brother, who elected to follow the scholar's life, may have been the wisest of the three (347). The book deals with the conflict of spirit and matter and the various complexities of the relationship between them. It is in a sense another dialogue between soul and body, and it reflects the Renaissance concern with the well-being of both inner and outer man.

Chapter 40

Two remarks in this chapter: "Do not trust any Moor; they are all deceitful" (359) and "Christians carry out their promises better than Moors" (360) further underline the racial and religious tensions of the times. Yet the remarks are curiously reminiscent of remarks made about an enemy in any era. In fact, one of the issues of the captive's tale is who and what can be trusted. Can the prisoners trust Zoraida? Can they trust the Murcian renegade who translates Zoraida's letter for them? Zoraida proves her good faith by drawing a cross at the end of her letter. The renegade's good character is established by his intention of remaining a Christian. Both are then traitors to their own countries and Zoraida to her own father. Nevertheless they are to be trusted, for they are Christians. Zoraida learned Christianity as a child from a slave woman. Her father believes she has renounced her Moorish faith because Christianity allows more immorality (375) —the Moor's side of the picture. Trust, then, is a relative matter dependent upon the side with which one's interests lie.

Religions have often provided the banners under which nations fight acquisitive wars. Christianity, with its concept of the church militant, has lent itself especially well to this role. Its dynamic character also may be seen in its conversions. By renouncing her home and her father for the sake of the Virgin Mary, Zoraida attests to the power of Christianity. She has much to lose and little to gain, but she is desirous of going with the captive and of becoming a Christian. Cervantes' Christian faith as well as his nationalism speak to us here in this chapter. By contrast, Hadji Murad, Zoraida's father, equates Christians and thieves (370). Cervantes does not believe him because Hadji Murad is a Moor, yet Zoraida, his Christian daughter, has had to steal from her father's coffers to ransom the prisoners.

Cide Hamete Benengeli, Cervantes' alter ego, is, interestingly enough, Arabic. Although doubtless of Mohammedan persuasion,

Cide represents a third and neutral faction in this struggle between Spain and the Moor, and such a narrator no one could
hope to imprison or to fine. Although Cide may in some instances
provide Cervantes with a convenient escape from political responsibility, in the episode of Zoraida it is not Cide but Cervantes
who speaks and attests to his own deep faith in the Christian
religion as well as to his own anti-Moorish prejudice, a prejudice
to be expected in a Spaniard of the day.

The captive's tale continues to provide us with windows
through which to view Spain of the Renaissance. That it follows
Don Quixote's discourse on arms versus letters is not chance, for
it illustrates with a specific example Don Quixote's thesis by
tracing the fortunes of one soldier through peril and hardship.
The continuity established by Cervantes establishes the structure
of the book, and the digressions turn out not to be digressions
at all.

Chapter 41

War and dissension often destroy compassion. Thus, Zoraida's
father is beside himself with grief, yet Zoraida is unable to offer
him much comfort. After all he is a Moor; she a Christian. One
by-product of the captive's tale is our increased awareness of the
meaning of war. Everyone in the tale lives in mortal terror of an
enemy or enemies. Moors fear Spaniards and Turks; Spaniards
fear Frenchmen, Turks, and Moors. Turks fear Christians from
all nations. Zoraida's father cannot believe that Christians will
grant him liberty (372). Zoraida herself remarks—to trick her
father—that Christians always lie and cheat Moors (366). Although in this chapter the company of Christians finally reaches
Spain, even here they are taken at first for Moors by a shepherd
boy and by the coastguard.

The desire for eminence, or whatever it may be that sets off a
conflict, colors all other aspects of the enemy. In both personal

and national conflicts we cannot help but believe ourselves at issue with monsters. So although Zoraida's father, to demonstrate his love, plucks his beard, tears his hair, and rolls on the ground, Zoraida remains firm in her intentions to flee to a foreign land with a man she scarcely knows. Among the warring factions in this chapter, only the French captain is moved to some compassion for an enemy (one suspects by Zoraida's beauty, which makes her somewhat less of a monster), into giving her forty crowns and allowing her to keep her clothes.

It is possible that this projection of a monster image upon the enemy is a means of denying this part of one's own make up— part of the virtuous pose each side assumes in war. In reading the captive's tale of a war now far removed from the passions, we can view in some perspective the assumption of belligerent attitudes which essentially serve only the most selfish and base of human aims. Religions themselves which claim to be the only true revelations further the same aims. Both Zoraida's religious attitude and that of her father are extremely self-centered, for neither sees any virtue in the other once Zoraida's religion is known. Yet since Cervantes is a Christian, Zoraida fares better than Hadji Murad in the long run.

Chapter 42

Cervantes' employment of the *deus ex machina* is perhaps nowhere more evident than in Chapter 42. Scarcely has the penniless captive finished his tale than a wealthy judge—accompanied by a beautiful daughter—appears at the inn. The judge is, it turns out, none other than the captive's brother. So with the arrival of the judge and with Don Ferdinand's change of heart, all troubles seem to be at an end.

Don Quixote with his redoubtable arms has had no hand in either solution. The priest is the one who brings the brothers together. Don Quixote can only spout a wordy welcome to the judge informing him that beauty is the pilot of both arms and letters—the judge representing letters—but the meaning of beauty to other people is lost upon him. He is especially blind in matters of emotional relationships—probably because this is a story of unfulfilled middle age. Incapable himself of forming a real emotional attachment, he idealizes a farm wench he scarcely knows and one far enough removed from his sphere to be a "safe" object of devotion. He shows very little understanding of the matchmaking going on at the inn under his very nose and accepts Dorothea's version of events which Sancho has already explained to him. His chivalric fantasies may be, one suspects, closely related to his thwarted sexual drives.

*　　*　　*

That Cervantes' chief aim is not satire of institutions, as some critics have thought, may be clearly seen in the figure of the judge or the priest. The court, the church, the penal system do, it is true, come under scrutiny, but Cervantes recognizes both good and evil qualities in them. Cervantes, however, is really interested in people. The judge is a high-minded and generous man, and the priest—despite his antic in maiden's clothes—is a man genuinely devoted to justice and to Don Quixote's welfare. Cervantes is mainly concerned with the inner man, with the quality of every man who ever cherished an ideal of human behavior. For a man like Cervantes, who had been imprisoned by his society, it is surprising that so little sense of injury creeps through. Rather, Cervantes sees that institutions are made by man and that until man learns about his own nature and how to deal with it, institutions will not improve. Perhaps Cervantes sees too that, of all evils, uncontrolled fantasy is the most wasteful and destructive.

Chapter 43

Cervantes makes further contrasts between the real and the ideal in this chapter. The love between Clara and her "mule lad" bears a superficial resemblance to Don Quixote's love for his Dulcinea. Like Don Quixote and Dulcinea, Clara and her lover have seen each other only from afar. Don Louis, like Don Quixote, has set out in costume on a mission for his beloved. Don Louis sings songs to his "shining star" as Don Quixote carves songs for Dulcinea on the bark of trees. But here the similarities end. Clara and Don Louis are moving toward a marriage in the real world despite the romance framework of their story. The two are well-matched, except for wealth and title, large barriers in Cervantes' time. Don Quixote's courtship, on the contrary, will continue *ad infinitum,* never proceeding beyond or receding from its present state. Ideality is a means of freezing or erasing time.

Yet the chapter turns away from the charming songs of young love to the plight of an old man, hanging by one arm from the window of an inn, tricked by two "demi-virgins"—as Cervantes delicately terms them. Time moves, we learn, even for those clinging to their ideal loves and the Grecian urn. Even Rocinante finally moves, stirred by the friendly advances of another horse. The ideal must sometimes give way to the relentless motion of the real. This same motion, or time, threatens even the love of Clara and Don Louis. Yet in his incomparable Dulcinea, Don Quixote finds comfort against these deprivations of time, a comfort which fortifies him in his confrontation with reality.

The scene also characterizes the increasing violence with which the world confronts Don Quixote. He is seen less and less often as he wishes to be seen and frequently becomes the butt of coarse jokes. Although he worries about his loss to the world as he hangs from the window, the world is drowned in sleep. His vision of himself as savior is shared by no one else. As the jokes increase in number and subtlety, the modern reader's compassion is aroused, even though the innkeeper asserts that we should pay no attention to Don Quixote since he is out of his mind (396). Still, Cervantes is able to point out—even to his contemporaries—that the odd inspires cruelty in the average man. We stamp, partly in fear, on psychological mutations. As Don Quixote's grotesqueness becomes more helpless and more aimless, it incurs the ungrateful mockery of the very world he thinks he serves with such devotion.

Chapter 44

Cervantes employs counterpoint in presenting the various episodes in this chapter. In brief they run as follows: (1) Four travelers arrive and find Don Louis whom they try to persuade to return to his father. (2) Don Quixote's help is sought in protecting the landlord. (3) Don Louis reveals his love to Clara's father. (4) The barber arrives and claims his basin and saddle.

The shifting back and forth between main and sub-plots enables us to compare various types of characters in similar situations. Don Louis' mission is no more concluded than Don Quixote's; neither wishes to return home, yet emissaries from home pursue both attempting to force them or to cajole them to return. Don Louis is as adamant as Don Quixote in his determination to see his mission through. Yet one is too young, the other too mad to bear the full responsibility for his decisions.

Nevertheless both pursue their goals with some success in this chapter. Don Louis enlists the aid of Clara's father, a vital move if he is to obtain his desire. And Don Quixote manages, partly by chance, it is true, to avenge himself on the landlord and his staff as well as to arrive at the satisfaction of seeing Sancho fight for his saddle. Curiously enough the very rules of chivalry, which have so often involved Don Quixote in bloody broils, enable him here to allow the landlord to be beaten to a pulp. First, he must have the Princess's permission to fight; then he remembers that as a knight he cannot fight squires. And for a whole page Cervantes leaves the upshot of the matter unsettled. While Don Louis speaks of his love to Clara's father, the landlord in the background continues to receive his beating. There is a strong suggestion of the picaresque hero avenging the innocent in this episode. Landlords were often little better than highway robbers—providing poor quarters and mediocre food for high prices. Whether consciously or unconsciously Don Quixote manages also to avenge his own treatment at the hands of Maritornes and the landlord's wife. By means of persuasion, however, not arms, Don Quixote finally makes peace, moved perhaps by a compassion the landlord does not know, and the guests pay their reckoning.

Cervantes does not indicate just how capable Don Quixote is of making mature decisions. How conscious he is of his role and how it can be applied are questions which are unanswerable, as they are for each human being. Which one of us can divide what is act from what is real? Given a long enough period of time the mask becomes the man, and our own chivalric counterpart— whether it be Amadis of Gaul, Merlin, or the Lady Guinevere —is the only reality. Cervantes gives the whole matter of play-acting close scrutiny throughout the book.

In the meantime, while Don Quixote is pursuing the course of reason and reconciliation, Sancho has taken up the profession of arms and is viciously attacking the barber. Sancho fights so well that Don Quixote considers knighting him. Sancho's motives for fighting are entirely materialistic, of course, yet for a moment the two protagonists have shifted roles. Not cowardice, but idealism, has forced Don Quixote to refrain from battle; not idealism, but worldly goods, have forced Sancho into the fray. Actually there is no basic change, although each has seemed to reverse his actions. Cervantes shows us here that a particular human act is meaningless apart from its motivating force. Sancho, although he fights, is still the same comfort-loving materialist, even inventing the word *baciyelmo* (basi-helmet) for the purpose of appeasing his master; and Don Quixote, although he negotiates peace, remains the mad idealist. (This point is especially significant in the light of those criticisms of the book which claim that Sancho and

Don Quixote gradually modify one another and change roles as the book progresses.)

It is also necessary to question the criticism which sees Don Quixote and Sancho as polar opposites. Raymond S. Willis in his article on Sancho as a prototype for characters in modern novels suggests that Cervantes proposes more than a simple dualistic scheme in *Don Quixote*. By calling the basin a "basi-helmet" Sancho "stands on the side of faith yet unconsciously defines the nature of human truth" (WS, 218), which rests in ambiguity. He is, therefore, Willis shows, essentially a modern hero; since he can *see* the basin, how can he believe it to be a helmet? His predicament is that of modern man and it delineates the central theme of the contemporary novel. Spanish literature of the Renaissance alone in its era created heroes who were, like Sancho, Celestina, or Cid, both ordinary human beings and "vast enough to encompass the destiny of Spain" (WS, 210)

Chapter 45

The question of the identity of Mambrino's helmet leads in this chapter to a regular epic *mêlée* after which peace is established, but it is broken again by a warrant issued for Don Quixote. The butt of the joke which runs throughout the chapter is ostensibly the barber who once owned the basin, but actually Cervantes, by means of mock heroic devices, holds the whole company up to ridicule.

That Don Quixote whose life is devoted to the righting of wrongs should be the instrument by which an innocent barber is about to be defrauded of his basin and pack saddle is high humor for the assembled company. Justice is sacrificed for the amusement of the group. Although Don Quixote himself is cautious about asserting the truth of anything connected with this enchanted castle, the others, led by Don Ferdinand, all state positively that the basin is a helmet and the pack saddle a harness.

Although Don Quixote becomes a source of amusement again for his companions, to the reader he appears, in a way, more rational than they. The encouragement of a madman in his wild fantasies seems a childish occupation by comparison with the aims of a life devoted to succouring the unfortunate.

The Holy Brotherhood itself also fares poorly in comparison with Don Quixote. It joins lustily in the fray, abetted by the innkeeper who turns out to be a member. But these "holy" men are not the ones to establish peace. Rather they fill the inn with slashings and punches. Don Quixote, imagining himself in Agramante's camp, is the one to cry out that all should sheathe their swords and that peace should be reestablished. It is this man that the Holy Brotherhood is attempting to arrest for highway robbery.

In a final twist of the irony Cervantes has his hero inform the brotherhood that they cannot arrest him, for he is a knight, and accordingly is subject to all sorts of "privileges and immunities" (410). What tailor was ever paid by a knight? What warden ever reimbursed? Here, of course, by assigning himself to a special category the hero becomes again the mad hero. It is now that the priest steps in to plead for Don Quixote's freedom on the basis of his insanity.

Yet the reader leaves the chapter reluctantly. Who has won? And what is reality? Organized society lends stability to existence, but perhaps the Don Quixotes too are needed, for without them there would be no one to reach for stars. Don Quixote's mistake lies in thinking that the trappings of knight errantry will automatically affect its virtues. Still, it is the priest and Don Ferdinand who reimburse the barber and the innkeeper and establish a final and lasting peace. Don Quixote is continually unable to effect any of his virtuous aims. The power of money, Cervantes frankly tells us, surpasses the most pious intentions. Yet Cervantes lingers with the idealism of his hero, leaving the description of the payments to the barber and innkeeper to the following chapter. In Chapter 45 we leave Don Quixote discoursing on the courage of a knight who will face four hundred troopers. The authenticity of Don Quixote is constantly plucking at the sleeve of even the

most practical-minded reader—an annoying reminder of his own
lost inwardness.

Chapters 46 and 47

The cage in which Don Quixote is transported toward home
is symbolic of all the antics other people are forced to perform
in Don Quixote's behalf. The enchantment is part of the act
which the barber and priest are compelled to play out if they are
to effect Don Quixote's return. So compelling is Don Quixote's
own role that others conform to his ways rather than making him
conform to theirs. Yet to the barber and priest their masks are
only temporary devices and their motivation that of love for an
old friend. Still we note that as Don Quixote has pursued his
travels scarcely anyone he has met has not been attracted by some
aspect of his chivalric act. Others are drawn as if by a tropism,
and their own latent chivalric interests arise from suppressed areas
of their minds.

At the conclusion of this section when the Canon discourses
on books of chivalry, the crux of Don Quixote's problem comes
to the fore. The Canon feels that the more a book resembles the
truth, the better the fiction, the fewer the impossibilities, the
fewer excesses. This is an academic judgment if ever there was
one, for fiction by its very definition is the antonym of truth.
Yet if the Canon wishes fiction to resemble truth, Don Quixote
wishes the fiction of chivalry to *be* truth. The Canon's basis of
reference is outward, Don Quixote's inward. Oppositions may be
reconciled only in the mind; in the physical world they remain
polarities. This section gives still another insight into the nature
of madness. Yet is the Canon any less mad in insisting that fiction
resemble truth and that the lone virtue of books of chivalry lies
in the opportunity they provide an author to display his virtuosity? Far better—one suspects—to assume the truth of chivalry

in the actions of one's life—even though by doing so one may be termed a holy madman.

Chapter 48

Cervantes takes the opportunity to poke sly fun at the academic world in this chapter. The priest and Canon agree that good drama must follow the rules—in particular, the unities of time, place, and action. They feel that people who flock to see plays which are grossly composed perform a sacrilege, and managers of playhouses are guilty of opportunism. What is needed, they say, is a critic or censor to examine all plays before they are performed. Instead playwrights try to adapt themselves to the requirements of the mob which pays them.

This accusation is directed principally against Lope de Vega, who often departed from classical norms to write comedies which were popular at the time (Cervantes himself had followed classical rules in his plays.) Lope de Vega had written on this point in several passages in his *Arte nuevo de hacer comedias en este tiempo* stating that he did not employ classical precepts for comedy because common taste did not demand them. The playwright was paid, he continued, to write foolishly in order to amuse the public (OB, 522).

Of some interest is the fact that in 1615 the Council of Castille created a censor who was to be concerned with the morality of plays. Had the literary censorship proposed by the canon in this chapter been allowed, harm certainly would have been done to the entire cause of the Spanish theater. (OB, 520-521)

So here again we find exposed in still another area the central polarity of the book—the division between the ideal and the real. The tragedy of the novel lies in the fact that the hero, like the canon with his censor, is unable to bridge the two. Only too late does he realize what his role should have been. Enclosed in his cage, Don Quixote has no chance to attack with his lance the vulgarity of bad art or to sweep away with his plume the dust and mold in the brain of the overzealous scholar.

The cage in which he returns home symbolizes above all Don Quixote's self-imposed shackles. Inwardly, although he prates of Amadis of Gaul's idealism, he makes certain that he will do nothing about it. His very armor is a cage which makes successful completion of his missions impossible. He is constantly imprisoning himself in futile arguments and misdirected quarrels. Never can he free himself for a real attack on injustice or untruth, and so it is no wonder that eventually his fellow man catches sight of the image the knight has of himself and provides literally the bars he has already inwardly erected. The pathos in the insecurity of this figure tugs at the reader, for perhaps his "sad countenance" stems not from others' actions but from his self-derision. That he is moved to surmount his doubt under the guise of knight proves only that knights, of all persons, are the most vulnerable, for in their fiction they strive for perfection. Don Quixote as he travels home, tied in his cage, has lived up only to his estimate of himself as impotent in all areas of human affairs. But Don Quixote does not entirely lose the vision of the knight as he should be: an ideal figure impressed on the reader's mind by means of its opposite.

Chapter 49

Goethe once wrote that the confusion of the real and the ideal never goes unpunished. Don Quixote's conversation with the Canon illustrates this confusion and the reason for his punishment, the hypocrisy of his approach to existence. Don Quixote is confronted at times by his own deception and self-deception. Sometimes he flagrantly uses his role to humor himself, as when in this chapter he insists to Sancho that he is enchanted and must remain in his cage. It seems that his main reason for finally agreeing to leave his cage is to relieve himself. Toward the end of this first book we find a tired knight quite willing to return to his village under the guise of enchantment. It is Sancho, not Don Quixote, who proposes new adventures. In his conversation with the Canon, Don Quixote remains content to talk of adventure, to talk of the glories of chivalry, and of the idealistic past.

Chapter 50

Cervantes has Sancho enter the debate between the Canon and Don Quixote only to illustrate once more Sancho's materialistic motives. Sancho's governorship seems to him a matter of "doing what he pleases" (443), and his ideals fall short of Don Quixote's—to be valiant, courteous, and to endure. Sancho's strengths lie in this world; Don Quixote's in the world of the spirit or mind. When the goatherd begins his story Sancho asks to be excused so that he may enjoy his pie in solitude.

* * *

When we speak of "problems" in connection with Don Quixote, we speak only of the reader's view of the man. Don Quixote himself would admit to no problems as we see in this chapter in his defense of books of chivalry. True he undergoes hardships, but these are experienced by all knights errant. All his faults are externalized so that his failures become the work of enchanters. Never does he admit to error of judgment. Sancho points out that enchantment usually paralyzes all bodily functions. To which Don Quixote replies—there are many kinds and fashions of enchantment. The serious intent of his mission must never be questioned, and if enchanters are not present, as in the episode of the fulling mills, he will resort to physical violence to subdue the disbelief of even his devoted servant.

Chapter 51

The goatherd's tale of the fickle Leandra is a fitting final digression in the 1605 *Quixote*. From the story of Marcela (also told by a goatherd) to the one of Leandra, the digressions have described various situations of people in love, and supply the conventional romance and pastoral elements of the tale, as opposed to the chivalric and the picaresque elements. The digressions are arranged as follows: Marcela scorns her lovers; Lucinda apparently thwarts Cardenio but later thwarts Don Ferdinand and accepts Cardenio; Don Ferdinand deserts Dorothea and later under pressure marries her; Camilla deceives her husband, Anselmo, who would test her faithfulness, then in penance becomes a nun— an episode that is directly the opposite of that involving Marcela. Then we have the devotion of Maria and the captive, followed by that of Clara and her mule boy. Obstacles to these two love affairs stem not from the lovers but from external influences— fathers and societal forces. We conclude with the goatherd's tale of Leandra who, thinking she has found her true love, runs off with Vincente only to be deserted by him. Eugenio retires, like Marcela, to the country—not to curse men but to spend his days despising women. Cervantes shows admirable insight into the plight of the deserted lover when Eugenio remarks that he despises his goat, Speckle, as a female even though she is the best in his flock—revealing his ambivalence towards Leandra in his feeling for Speckle.

In brief, these digressions may be seen to run the gamut of love, from Marcela who victimizes her lovers to maintain her independence, to Don Ferdinand who victimizes two women to satisfy his lust, to Camilla and Anselmo who victimize each other, to two lovers thwarted at first by society, and finally to Leandra, who, because of her frivolity, makes victims of Anselmo and Eugenio. All of these episodes of physical love are set against the backdrop of a hero bent on a spiritual mission.

Chapter 52

It is fitting that Don Quixote's final adventure in the 1605 *Quixote* is an attempt to rescue a damsel who is in reality an image of the Virgin Mary carried by a procession to invoke rain which has not fallen in Don Quixote's district for a year. The question that we might wish to ask after Don Quixote's assault on the rain makers is—does the Virgin Mary require rescuing from the Catholic faith? Yet obviously Cervantes a devout Catholic— sees the matter in a different light. Once again a dominant chord of the book is sounded—that of the holy madman. In all good faith Don Quixote rushes to the aid of the lady in black—yet how misdirected his energy proves to be. Nothing is achieved but a good laugh or, perhaps more accurately, a good cry—at least from Sancho who thinks his master is dead. Yet, ironically, in this last adventure Don Quixote reaches the peak of his career—the defense of the lady of his religion whom all knights are bound to defend. Her identity, however, is unknown to him, and in her defense he is knocked to the ground as if dead.

Had Cervantes not lived ten years to return to his tale, Don Quixote would have remained in the grave to which the epitaph at the end of this book assigns him. The book itself can be judged a highly amusing yet thoughtful picaresque tale. But it is episodic and, despite threads of continuity and progression, does not really proceed in any large measure toward the self-realization of the hero. The Don Quixote who returns to his village is essentially the same Don Quixote who left—only a little more distracted, a little more weary. Nothing is really concluded, and Cervantes himself must have sensed it, for he proposes the publication of a third expedition. Just how it increases our understanding of the knight and what further subtleties are introduced will be discussed later, but it does offer a conclusion which shows the book in the final analysis to be the purest example of the tragic genre and not, as Book I would have us believe (as the company roars over Don Quixote's fight with the goatherd in the last chapter), the purest of picaresque comedies permeated with a pathos felt mainly, I suspect, by those who, like Cervantes himself, are prey to a thwarted idealism.

Yet behind the comedy lies a deeper meaning which it has been the purpose of this study to bring out. As Bruce Wardropper states, "the primary intuition of the novel is the blurring of boundary lines" (WARD, 11). It is this ambiguity, this defiance of absolute truth which Cervantes suggests. 'Good judgment' depends on one's perspective and on one's purpose. Dogmatism and self-assurance are seen again and again to fail those who profess them. Cervantes tells us that mankind, like Don Quixote, is doomed to mingle truth with fiction, for our perspectives can be at best merely imperfect ones.

Don Quixote, 1615

Dedication

Not until 1615, ten years after the publication of **Part One**, did Cervantes send his new patron, the Count of Lemos, the second volume of his knight's adventures. The typical Renaissance dedication pretends to spurn worldly rewards while at the same time subtly hinting at their importance. Thus Cervantes tells his patron that his first aim has been to purge the world of an imposter who has been masquerading as the real Quixote. But he also informs the Count that fame and honor (as rector of a college, a position offered him by the Emperor of China) mean nothing to him because the Emperor has mentioned no salary. The Count, on the contrary, supplies Cervantes with bread and butter, a point which Cervantes emphasizes by means of a pretty compliment in which the Count is compared favorably with emperors and monarchs. But there is an implied threat, too: other important persons, as far away as China, have approved Cervantes' work. Other patrons would not be difficult to find. Cervantes does not fail to say, moreover, that he is at work on *The Travels of Persiles and Sigismunda,* a new volume (which will, of course, need a dedication.) Thus Cervantes dispenses for the moment with the heady idealisms of Don Quixote in favor of the shrewd practicality of Sancho Panza.

Prologue

Thomas Mann warns the reader of *Don Quixote* (COL, 53) not to forget that the 1615 *Quixote* was composed in order to rescue the honor of the 1605 *Quixote,* which had been endangered by the appearance of Avellaneda's plagiarism. This book had been seized upon by the reading public although it lacked the depth and diversity of Cervantes' original. "A certain literary frigidity" of the 1615 *Quixote* may, Mann points out, be due in part to Cervantes' need to prove distinction. In fact, Cervantes loses no time in approaching the subject of plagiarism.

In the first sentence of the prologue he introduces the new theme, that of the sham *Don Quixote* of an imposter writer. Although he pretends to take the matter lightly, Cervantes is clearly disturbed. "Let his sin be his punishment" (467) are only words, for the entire prologue (as well as later passages) is given over to berating this unnamed enemy. His method of attack is of particular interest. After some opening defensive remarks, Cervantes branches out into two devastating parables. In each the central figure is a madman. We see that madness and genius are indeed bedfellows and that what divides the two is that genius accomplishes in the end a meaningful rapport with others. The madman in Seville, who inflates dogs, is employed in a difficult and senseless business. Cervantes is quite willing to put himself into the shoes of the madman and his works into the category of inflated dogs if only to make his point that even such aimless activity is difficult. He lays no claim to genius, only to inflating dogs, an understatement intentionally displaying his modesty. Implied is the point that his enemy's talents are of inferior quality to the madman's. The imposter is a bystander who cannot even inflate dogs.

Cervantes adds to this insult to the imposter's skill in the second parable, which conceals a threat. Dropping stones on dogs, especially stones as hard as bad books, is a dangerous occupation, for the owner of the dog may be watching and beat the madman to a pulp.

Of particular significance is the choice of two madmen to represent writers. Don Quixote, too, is a madman. Author and hero are, as Cervantes later tells us, one. The idea held by the writer and given birth in book form by him must of necessity be born in solitude. Its reception in the world at large is what determines its author's madness or sanity. The relationship of the creative artist to his audience is always an ambiguous one. The attempt to communicate is often only half successful, and there abound misunderstandings and misreadings. Thus the artist's relation to so-called reality is constantly called into question. Cervantes, in identifying with his hero, is simply restating the problems faced by any creative thinker in his society. Perhaps it is necessary to relinquish a bit of reality, to become a madman at least temporarily, if one is to establish a new and better reality. It is this kind of idealism which permeates *Don Quixote*. The relationship between what is and what ought to be is seen to be full of complexities and problems.

*　*　*

At the end of the Prologue Cervantes returns to the theme of the dedication. The Count of Lemos has not been forgotten through all the chatter about madmen. The imposter may be rich, but Cervantes does not care a straw. A poor man has his honor. Nobility may not be entirely obscured by poverty. But still, nobility would shine brighter without poverty, and more books are on the way and more flattering dedications to be written. The Count of Lemos would do well to see that Cervantes is at least as well paid as his dishonest imitator.

Chapter 1

Cervantes here relates the barber's tale of a madman, which augments the parables of the two madmen in the Prologue. Don Quixote is not blind to the barber's implication that he, Don Quixote, is like the madman. He says, in effect, "I know you see me as this madman, but I do not claim to be Neptune, as he does. All I want is to change the world." So although he says he understands the barber, in essence he seems to understand only little of the barber's story. As Neptune, in speaking to Jupiter, reveals his insanity, so Don Quixote, in his conversation with the barber, reveals his own, for who can take seriously his aim of reviving chivalry?

There is a basic difference, however, between Don Quixote and Neptune. Neptune sees his function as only that of rainmaker, in the actual sense. Don Quixote, in saying he will "rain when he pleases," changes the original, literal meaning of Neptune's statement to a figurative one, meaning I will do my good works when I please. At least his intentions and purposes are socially oriented. Neptune has concern only for making rain; Don Quixote is concerned with industry, virtue, valor, and arms. Nor does Don Quixote consider the literal, physical revival of chivalry as an end in itself. Always, as in this chapter, the description of the physical labors of the knight are followed and overshadowed by an awareness of the virtues of the chivalrous life.

*   *   *

It is fitting that the first chapter of the 1615 *Quixote* should open with a discussion of politics during the reunion of the priest, the barber, and Don Quixote. They speak of ways of governing, of correcting abuses, and of reforming customs (471). Don Quixote thinks reform can only be achieved by exchanging one age for another. Behind this belief lies the conviction, founded

in the late Middle Ages (See MAR, 106-107), that since the state
is something men organize, not something given, men can reor-
ganize it. *Nature* is the original order of things founded by God;
experience, on the other hand, is forged by man. This discussion
of the need for reform, then, provides the rationale for the practice of arms which Don Quixote is shortly to take up once again,
though in a manner more foolish than constructive.

*   *   *

Part of the depth of the priest's role in the book comes from
his (and the barber's) partial commitment to Don Quixote's own
Weltanschauung. Although they have agreed beforehand not to
touch on matters of knight-errantry, both are itching to do so, and
once the subject is broached, the priest is delighted with the
conversation. The functions of priest and of Don Quixote are
basically similar, as both their philosophies and missions stem
from myth. To resurrect Christ in the hearts of men is a task
not unlike Don Quixote's attempt to resurrect the knight-errant.
Both priest and Don Quixote have holy and high-minded goals.
As Ivan Karamazov knew, the actual return of Christ would be
greeted with the derision of organized authority. The physical
resurrection of the knight-errant is greeted likewise with derision.
Don Quixote has yet to learn the lesson the church has always
known: Myth can serve only as a stimulus to the present, never
as a replacement for it. To reanimate the past is impossible, and
the attempt to do so leads only to the insanity of the creator.
Don Quixote as a knight in armor is an anachronism, although
the virtues promoted by the system of chivalry are not.

One of the underlying subjects of this book is the relationship between past and present. This is complicated by the fact
that we are speaking of a past (the fictional chivalric world) which
never was a past. If our image of past events we have actually
experienced is inexact, how much more distorted is an apocryphal
past seen through the eyes of countless writers of chivalric lore
and, in turn, through the Renaissance reader, Don Quixote. The
value system we are concerned with, then, has its basis in the
fantasy world of the human mind. How well it works in practice

has been seen (for example, the Andrew episode). And yet the values of Don Quixote are essentially Christian values, the same ones propounded by the priest. The central metaphors behind these values are the Christ figure and the knight. Chivalry sprang directly from a Christian culture. And yet the use of force, which it sanctions, is different from the appeal to human conscience made by Christianity. Christianity, in theory, sees that violence breeds revenge, and that as soon as Don Quixote's back is turned the farmers will continue to lay their whips upon their hapless Andrews. Furthermore, if human conscience cannot be moved by reason and by example, it cannot be moved at all, and our actions must, therefore, be defensive.

Chapter 2

That Don Quixote is not immune to vanity is shown by his great interest in the public's opinion of his feats. For example, he questions Sancho carefully about people's reactions to him in the village. He is particularly sensitive about his image in the minds of others and in the book that has been written about him. This mirroring of self or the question of identity is to be a dominant theme throughout this entire book. When he learns that people see him as "mad but amusing," "valiant but unfortunate," "well-mannered but presumptuous" (484), he falls back upon the common defense that virtue is always persecuted and compares himself to Caesar, Alexander, and Hercules, who also received criticism and abuse. What others may think does not change his opinion of himself.

Ironically, the persons Don Quixote does overcome are his niece and the housekeeper. All their attempts to keep Sancho out of his master's room fail, and they have no recourse, despite Don Quixote's vows to aid all maidens in distress. As parodies of ladies of a knight's household, they fill the role. Their language is coarse, their tasks menial, their dress ordinary. In contrast to the ladies of chivalric lore, they do not aid and abet their lord in his adventures, but attempt to stop him. We see them struggling to hold the door against Sancho, pure mockery of the typical chivalric tale.

Chapter 3

Cervantes introduced Sampson Carrasco, the Bachelor, in part to satirize the product of the Renaissance university. Carrasco, even more than the priest, encourages the Don in his mad fantasies but from different motives. Whereas the priest half shares the Don's fantasy world, Sampson Carrasco is moved by his mischievous disposition, by his love of the practical joke. "Of great intelligence" (486), he does not consider the real import of Don Quixote's mission. One disciple of genuine intelligence could perhaps have turned the mission into a fruitful one, could have encouraged a process of sublimation in the Don whereby the ideals of knighthood could have been achieved in a more successful manner. It is worth noticing that among all the cures mentioned for the Don not one provides a realistic substitute for his knight-errantry.

Through the Bachelor, Cervantes satirizes the literate university graduate in his ivory tower. Never does Sampson come to grips with the problem of Don Quixote's madness. He plays with it like a child with a new toy. Furthermore, his understanding of the first volume of *Don Quixote* seems limited to its externals. He informs Don Quixote of the number of copies printed, of the place of publication, of some of the episodes, and of criticisms he has heard. But to its real import he is blind as he is blind to the real intention of its hero.

The behavior of Sampson introduces the theme of playacting, which is to be a major one throughout the book. The Knight of the Mirrors, the Duke and the Duchess, and finally Don Antonio Moreno create some of the most elaborate deceptions practiced on Don Quixote. They represent various modulations on this theme. In the final analysis, the perpetrators are seen as less noble than Don Quixote himself, although all are engaged in a deception. For his own amusement, simply to pass time, Sampson pretends to take Don Quixote seriously and later assumes the role of knight himself for the same reason. The leisured classes, the sophisticates, alone adopt this attitude toward Don Quixote. Only when Sampson is unhorsed does his intention lose its frivolity—but not its self-centeredness—for personal revenge now takes the place of entertainment, neither one worth the time and energies of a bachelor "of great intelligence."

As A. A. Parker shows, the frivolity of Sampson can best be seen by contrasting it to Don Quixote's nobility. Sampson has been willing to deceive Don Quixote for the fun of it. But after the encounter with the Knight of the Mirrors, Don Quixote, rather than believe that his friend Carrasco has deceived him, places the blame for the Knight's resemblance to Sampson on magic. (PF, 12)

Don Quixote is a kind of mirror wherein each character in the book finds the image of himself. Sampson sees a parody of the Don; Sancho sees a man that he can love; the priest sees a man that he can both love and parody. Don Quixote also has the opportunity to mirror himself, for Mia Gerhardt points out (GER, 47) that he is the hero of his *own* novel already published.

Chapter 4

Cervantes is able at several points in the 1615 *Quixote* to make the first part of his novel an element in the second part. In Chapter 4 Cervantes creates the opportunity to answer the critics of his first book. He uses Carrasco to summarize the criticisms and Don Quixote and Sancho to answer them (for who could know more than they of the events in Book I?) In Chapter 3 Don Quixote was worried when Carrasco mentions the matter of the digressions. (It is noteworthy that Cervantes attempts few actual digressions in the 1615 *Quixote*.) And Sancho explains the factual omissions. Thus each is again relegated to his role: Don Quixote's concern with form and Sancho's with content, paralleling their larger roles in the novel.

More important, however, is Don Quixote's decision to set out again within eight days. In fact, since we learn that Cide (whose only interest is profit) (494) is searching for Book II, it behooves Don Quixote to start out soon. (It is a minor irony that Don Quixote's avowed intention is to protect and succor the unfortunate, not to augment the income of an Arab.) Sancho's mind, like Cide's, is of a practical turn, for he stipulates that he will do no more fighting and accept no more beatings on this new adventure.

Chapter 5

The conversation between Sancho and his wife as well as providing amusement provides interesting insights into human psychology. Although the translator of Cide doubts Sancho's ability to carry on at such a subtle level, the student of human behavior sees typical reactions in the scene. The translator (like Sampson Carrasco, who has been worried in Chapter 4 about getting the name of Dulcinea into four stanzas) is no doubt a scholar of plodding disposition. For Sampson, the form of the verse must be exact; for the translator even human nature must portray a stupid consistency. Riquer points out that Sancho has developed and sharpened almost without Cervantes' being aware of it. As a result, Cervantes felt he had to explain the change in Sancho, which he did through the translator, who says he considers the chapter apocryphal because of Sancho's new-found subtleties (RIQ, 133).

Actually, as any armchair psychologist knows, we often play the role of the person we identify with or admire, particularly in our relations with those who admire us. And yet often that

role, to the impartial observer, is viewed with suspicion or amusement because it does not seem authentic. Thus, Sancho's intentions to become a governor and to raise the social level of his
family, in particular that of his daughter, caricature the intentions of Don Quixote, who desires anything but social eminence.
Sancho goes so far as to call his wife a "creature" (499) and to
correct her malapropism (502) in the same superior manner that
Don Quixote takes with Sancho.

Yet perhaps we can look even further. The chivalric system
is a caste system, and Don Quixote has not failed to maintain his
social superiority to Sancho. The role of the squire is an inferior
one, which both Don Quixote and Sancho are aware of. In an-
nouncing to his wife his intention of a second journey as squire
to Don Quixote, he is able to face his inferior role only if he
maintains the hope of improving his status. Her apparent rejection of his dream of governorship, sounding strangely like Sancho
himself in other portions of the book, can be interpreted either
as an "I love you as you are" statement or as an awareness of the
real purpose of Sancho's mentioning the governorship, a good
excuse for his second journey. Being squire to a madman takes
a good deal of explanation, both to oneself and to one's wife.
Thus Sancho is forced to rationalize, to insist that his squiring
will lead to a governorship, and his anger with Teresa increases
with her dogged and perhaps calculated misunderstanding of his
reasoning. Such remarks as "Keep to your own station, Sancho"
(499) and "I've always been a lover of equality" provoke Sancho
to yell "devil" and "creature" at his wife in a fury at being misunderstood. Although practical-minded and determined to look
out for his wages on this journey, Sancho has only one real
motive for accompanying Don Quixote, his love for his master.
It is, however, far easier to tell Teresa that his motive for going is
material gain in which she and their family will share. Her frus-
trating refusal to play along with his ploy is what provokes his
wrath.

Chapter 6

In vain Don Quixote's housekeeper and niece attempt to dissuade him from his new adventure. The amusing relationship between niece and uncle, in which the niece is depicted by Don Quixote as a young ninny, is a parody of the uncle-nephew relationship in the chivalric romance, in which the nephews rather than dissuading their uncles assisted them, even took their places in the lists, in return for the shelter and protection offered them. No such mutual arrangement exists between Don Quixote and his relative.

Don Quixote's defense of knighthood indicates that despite his chivalric "madness", he possesses on certain issues in other areas an excellent sense of reality. In exploring the four pedigrees of mankind, he maintains that virtue and liberality are the only claims to greatness any family can have. Genealogies are meaningless without these qualities. Two ways of achieving honor are through letters and through arms, through either spiritual or physical means. Knighthood is for him essentially a means of reaching toward the virtues that all men should seek, regardless of their birth.

Through such speeches as these, the real meaning of Don Quixote's adventures becomes apparent, and it is for this reason that Cervantes entitles it "one of the most important chapters in this entire history." Only by keeping Don Quixote's basic purpose in mind can we see beyond the artifice of his chivalric mode. Such passages impress us with the pathos of a man who possesses high aims and yet becomes involved in a kind of child's play (moral maturity combined with psychological adolescence.)

Chapter 7

The Bachelor, Sampson Carrasco, is perhaps the central figure in this chapter, in which Don Quixote and Sancho finally determine to set forth. When the housekeeper appeals to Carrasco for help in restraining her master, the Bachelor makes a slip and prescribes the wrong prayer to her, later supporting his error by citing his bachelor's degree. Cervantes never fails to exploit in ever way possible the chicanery of this product of the university. Even his first name is a delusion—a Sampson who is related in name only to the Biblical Samson, a Sampson who is no tower of strength.

Nor is he free from self-deception. Having assured the housekeeper that he will help to dissuade Don Quixote from taking his journey, he goes to offer the knight his services as squire. Actually, Sampson thinks that his offer is part of a plan he and the Priest have hatched to thwart Don Quixote's second adventure. However, it is more a means of gratifying Sampson's own desire to play at chivalry. Like many others in the book, Carrasco hankers after the trappings of Don Quixote's role while lacking any understanding of its real import. Sampson's intelligence touches only the shapes and forms of things, never the substance.

Chapter 8

Sancho proclaims himself as a most virtuous person because he believes in God and the tenets of the Church, and hates Jews, but the twisted thinking of his remark is all too apparent. No society can achieve the perspective necessary to see that its hatreds are as relative as its allegiances. In another age a person is "virtuous" if he hates Communists. Furthermore, Sancho is a Christian, and Christian churches (as we learn on the next page from Don Quixote) preach love. Sancho's remark makes the paradoxes of organized society and religion become uncomfortably clear.

As the pair moves on toward El Toboso, Don Quixote informs Sancho that the desire to win fame is so great with some people that they seek it in all kinds of unorthodox ways, through evil deeds as well as good ones. When he suggests that the fame of saints may be greater than that of knights-errant, Sancho inquires why he and Don Quixote do not then turn saints.

In fact, the whole question of altruism lies at the core of this chapter. It is suggested that self-interest (fame) is at the bottom of good deeds, even perhaps those of the saints. Don Quixote argues, however, that deeds (such as that of the man who standing beside an emperor would cast himself from a high building) are fruitless and that winning fame is meaningless unless they are combined with an active interest in others. The chapter thus defines what we mean by sublimation—to turn base desires to higher aims so that others may benefit. The saints and the knights-errant are among those who have "sublimated" successfully.

Chapter 9

Don Quixote is in high spirits at the prospect of viewing the peerless Dulcinea. After a crushing defeat, he would have been all too ready to see the parish church as Dulcinea's palace or its priest as the lord of a castle, but since he has suffered no defeat in this episode, he promptly identifies the church. It has become clear it is frustration that leads to Don Quixote's attacks of madness.

In fact, Don Quixote in this scene is lucid enough to recognize Sancho's jesting, warning him to speak respectfully of Dulcinea. But when Sancho insists that he no more than his master has ever seen the lady, Don Quixote holds doggedly to Sancho's lie (just as disrespectful to Dulcinea) about his visit to El Toboso, which Cervantes describes in the 1605 *Quixote,* telling Sancho that there are times for jokes and times when jokes are out of place. Don Quixote meets any threat to his ideal world with instant reinforcement of his mad fantasy.

Chapter 10

In his soliloquy near the opening of this chapter, Sancho admits that in looking for Dulcinea he would be a madman looking for "nothing." No one, he tells us, will cause him to search for "a cat with three legs" (526). He is fully aware that his master is a raving lunatic, one who mistakes white for black and black for white. Why not substitute, then, a peasant girl for Dulcinea? Don Quixote has done just the opposite; he has substituted Dulcinea for a peasant girl.

Sancho's motives are practical ones, to save himself unnecessary trouble where other people are concerned; Don Quixote's motives in becoming a knight are to involve himself with the troubles of other people, to accept the challenge of helping those in distress. Still, because of his mad fiction, he, too, is looking for "nothing," and Sancho is "right"—"neither I nor my master have ever seen her" (526). The difference is that Sancho for practical reasons degrades the ideal Dulcinea whereas Don Quixote in his re-creation of chivalry transforms a common peasant girl into a "lady."

At the same time Sancho "sees" three distinguished ladies whereas Don Quixote "sees" three coarse peasant girls (See RIQ, 137). Cervantes has apparently reversed the situation we find in the 1605 *Quixote.* However, is the situation of Part I actually reversed; have the roles really been exchanged?

Sancho is perfectly aware of his deception; he does not really *see* three ladies. Don Quixote, in contrast, remains inwardly constant to the ideal Dulcinea; Sancho's lie is far more compelling

for Don Quixote than the girls mounted on their burros. " 'And
to think I did not see all this, Sancho,' he cries" (532). The motives of knight and squire are what differentiate them, not the
roles they happen to play at a particular moment. For Sancho
the end of all action is to discover practical solutions; however,
Don Quixote, like Pygmalion, would reform the crude material
of the world, despite practical inconveniences. To these ends the
two characters remain steadfast, and even though the deceptions
of Sancho and others may seem to imitate those of Don Quixote,
they imitate them only superficially or ironically.

Don Quixote remains incredulous, and he cannot believe that
the three peasant girls really are Dulcinea and two of her maidens,
nor that the she-asses are hackneys. He becomes even more incredulous as Sancho showers courtesies upon the girls. The only
possible explanation for Don Quixote is that enchanters must be
at work; enchantment is an artifice, as Richard Predmore shows
in discussing *Don Quixote,* through which man reconciles the
worlds of being and seeming. (PRE, 52)

Cervantes introduces a new element in the 1615 edition of
Quixote. He portrays Don Quixote as more objective about the
nature of his quest. One wonders now if he himself always believes that enchanters are at work or if he is simply playing the
game. In one sense, the game has become one of mutual delusions in which both Don Quixote and Sancho are urging each
other on for different ends. The whiff of raw garlic from Dulcinea may be the work of enchanters; however, one cannot help
but feel in this part of the book that Don Quixote is now even
more aware of his role as an actor in a play in which enchanters
also have parts. In the 1605 *Quixote* his actions were unrehearsed.
Author and hero have now had time to meditate, Don Quixote
in his bed at home, Cervantes for ten years in his native Spain.
The new Quixote who emerges is more sophisticated, more philosophical, and more disillusioned. He can perhaps recognize that
truths are fashioned, not grown on trees, and that a Dulcinea
enchanted and smelling of raw garlic is as useful to his purpose
as one roped with pearls and smelling of ambergris. Sancho hides
his amusement at Don Quixote's gullibility, but unknown to
Sancho, Don Quixote may have hidden his disbelief in the higher

interests of his belief. In this scene we have no real proof of this new sophistication of the hero, only the mounting suspicion that Don Quixote has taken a hard look at his mission. His moments of madness do still occur in the development of his new rationality, but he now views the sad and cruel world around him on its own terms. In *Don Quixote's Profession* Mark Van Doren shows that in both parts of the book Don Quixote was an actor, a skillful actor, who wrote his own play and kept himself at stage center. Van Doren sees that his purpose was not to pretend but to understand. So when, at the end of the book, Don Quixote finds that ideals can take on flesh and blood, he abandons his quest, for having assumed physical form the ideal ceases to be ideal.

That Don Quixote is capable of idealisms is not surprising; that his means for attaining them are still as ineffective as they were in the 1605 *Quixote* is clear; but his view of the reality with which he has to cope, the reality of peasant girls, of the nature of Sancho and of the rest of the world around him has now come into focus. His helpless acceptance of this reality, for "he could think of no remedy," (532) is what demarcates the later part from the earlier part of the novel. This acceptance grows to the point where Don Quixote in later scenes with the Duke and Duchess behaves almost like a robot, performing mechanically the functions he had once performed with spontaneous enthusiasm.

Chapter 11

That Don Quixote is aware that Sancho is lying about Dulcinea is suggested in his amusing reproach of Sancho for saying that she had eyes like pearls. (533) He appears to believe that Sancho's confusion with the image is simply a slip, but had Sancho really seen Dulcinea's peerless eyes, could he, Don Quixote wonders, have compared them with pearls? The Renaissance lyric convention comparing features of the loved one's face to various exotic objects and flowers is, of course, partly the object of the

satire here. But when Don Quixote tells Sancho to transfer the
pearls from her eyes to her teeth, he jests with Sancho in the way
that Sancho has often jested with him, revealing a sense of humor
which so often in previous scenes he has lacked. He is answering
Sancho's attempt at deception in kind. Nor does it really matter
now to Don Quixote whether or not Sancho or anyone else has
seen Dulcinea, for he has come to recognize that his mission ex-
tends beyond earthly beauty and worldly rewards. Nevertheless,
the game between Sancho and Don Quixote goes on, each playing his role, each thinking the other naive, and each in dead
earnest about reaching his ultimate goal. And although Don
Quixote's disillusionment is growing, he is at this point able to
bring some humor to bear upon the situation.

Don Quixote's discernment of the difference between appearance and reality is put to a real test with the wagon of players. Only momentarily is he deceived; almost immediately he
recovers his senses, remarking, "appearances are not always to be
trusted." (535) For the knight of 1605 this would have been an
unthinkable statement. All the components of life are loaded on
the wagon—Death, Love, Emperor, Devil, Angel—yet Don
Quixote's final pronouncement is to call them phantoms. In fact,
the players seem to affect chiefly the animals, Rocinante and
Dapple, rather than knight and squire; Rocinante is frightened
by the clown and Dapple by the Devil. Yet a central question
is raised in this chapter. Do the roles the actors play differ from
Don Quixote's role? Does Don Quixote reject them because he
sees himself mirrored in them, or is there a subtle difference
between the two pretenses? Perhaps one clue lies in the detail that
the player knight wore no headpiece, only a hat with plumes. In
other words, the mission of these actors is secular, not holy. Although they play *The Parliament of Death,* they only play it—do
not live it. Their costumes may be removed, their own personal-
ities assumed. Don Quixote, on the other hand, would admit to
no "costume" and assumes no foreign personality. When we speak
of his "role" we speak of it in terms of his life's purpose. The
players of Angulo El Malo are by comparison engaged in child's
play—mere pretense. They devote to their roles only the brief
hour they "strut" upon the stage whereas Don Quixote devotes

his life to his role. Nevertheless, the title of the play suggests that all roles are played in "the parliament of death," that even Don Quixote in the end must remove his costume and assume the earth from which he sprang. Furthermore, time is relative, and the amount of time spent on the stage does not necessarily measure the quality or impact of the performance. This discomforting thought, as well as the reminder that all roles end in the parliament of death may be the reason for Don Quixote's rejection of the players as "phantoms." Such ambiguities as these can permeate the apparently most simple episode. Furthermore, these players seem better equipped to defend themselves against death than Don Quixote himself, whose horse bolts and who, in all his armor, knows he is no match for men armed with stones.

Chapter 12

Once the players are gone and Don Quixote and Sancho settled down to supper, the knight defends acting for its great value in holding up a mirror to life, in educating people. He himself makes a comparison between acting and life. Once his rivals are off stage he appears to believe that what upset him were the flight of Rocinante, the threats to Dapple's safety, and the troupe's resistance to his attempt at revenge. Yet, as we have seen, Don Quixote has a large store of rationalizations for his various failures and humiliations. Unable to cope with the professional actor, Don Quixote has called him "phantom." For a moment Don Quixote has felt the loneliness of the amateur, the outsider, thrust into competition with professionals.

The nature of the play was, of course, a matter of much importance for the Renaissance, and particularly for Cervantes, who was himself both playwright and actor. The Shakespearean metaphor: "All the world's a stage" reflects the very central concern of the Renaissance with the nature of man. However, Sancho's remark that he has heard the comparison before also serves to mock this imagery which had become little more than a literary cliché by the seventeenth century. [In fact, the concept of *theatrum mundi* goes back, as Ernst Curtius indicates, to Plato's *Laws,* and as a result of the *Policraticus,* where it again appears, was widely used in the Middle Ages. (CUR, 138-144)]

Don Quixote's thoughts on roles and on plays are typical of the interests of the times. It was an era in which life, rather than afterlife, was the central issue. Thus the nature of man's role and the ways and means of acting out a life, were matters of primary stress. Man was on stage, so to speak, not (as in the more austere theology of the time) waiting in the wings to make his appearance in Hell or Heaven.

Sancho's metaphor comparing life to a game of chess expresses a more worldly idea. At the end of the game pawn and knight are swept into a bag with all the other pieces, and pieces are moved by 'players,' just as roles are assumed by actors.

And yet even animals, says Cervantes in conclusion, can put men and their roles to shame, for the friendship between Rocinante and Dapple is such that few men (in mock heroic vein) except some in classical myths, have attained such loyalty.

Chapter 13

The Knight of the Mirrors and his squire, who next appear, serve to underline Cervantes' point about the nature of the arts and of plays. The device of disguise, as used in Renaissance literature, is at best sheer poetic license. That Sancho could not recognize Thomas Cecial first because of the dark and later because of a false nose is hardly credible. Yet the reader is willing for the sake of the scene to suspend his disbelief. Furthermore, the ground has been prepared for Sancho to accept Cecial as the Squire of the Wood. Constant association with Don Quixote has made knight-errantry a real mode of existence for Sancho, and he confronts the new squire in dead earnestness. It is ironical that whereas Don Quixote has seen the players in the previous episode for what they are, Sancho in this scene is tricked by an old friend. Don Quixote's mystique has led to disillusionment whereas Sancho's naiveté has developed into a mystique. In fact, Sancho has arrived at a position where he is ready to believe, if only reality will supply him with the mysteries he longs for. Despite his recognition that his master is mad, he somehow is also sure that his governorship is a distinct possibility. Within the framework of reality, chivalry, like a religion, offers its mysteries to dress up the everyday world. Mystery and miracle, as Ivan Karamazov suggested, are necessary to any popular theology. Sancho is not so much deceived as desirous of being deceived. He could wish that knights-errant were all-powerful, that giants existed to be conquered, that damsels abounded to grant favors, and that governorships of isles grew on trees. Thus his conversation with the Squire of the Wood, although full of his usual down-to-earth imagery, is overshadowed by the fantasy of the chivalric romance. In fact, both men are partially deceived by the fiction in which they participate and accept without questioning their roles as squires.

Chapter 14

Although a careful look at Sampson Carrasco shows him to be secretly enamored of the knightly role himself, Don Quixote is also glad to have an excuse to don armor and to set forth on an adventure. Yet Don Quixote's behavior in this chapter is something less than ideal. He takes unfair advantage of his opponent whose horse has stopped and whose lance is askew; after the fight he might have killed Sampson had not Sancho intervened. Don Quixote's recent frustrations have once more forced him into a fantasy world. Humiliated by the wagon of players, he is ready, like a child, to avenge himself on life if he can. The circumstances of his madness are consistent: a mounting frustration capped by a threat to his self-esteem. Only when defeat after defeat has impressed upon him the uselessness of his escape into fantasy does he finally give up this defense mechanism. Throughout the 1615 *Quixote* we can see his disillusionment growing despite his concomitant desire to continue the game.

The gloom surrounding Sampson and his squire as they depart is caused not only by the bachelor's broken ribs but by his shattered self-image. Like Don Quixote, the bachelor desires to achieve some real stature through a successful knight-errantry, if not in the eyes of others at least in his own eyes. He and Don Quixote are parallel figures. It is all child's play, and rules may be broken if no one is watching. God is not a heavenly umpire, Cervantes shows us with humanistic emphasis.

Chapter 15

Although Sampson sees clearly that the madman who cannot help himself is madder than the madman by choice, he seems by his defeat to become fixed in his role. Ironically, Don Quixote's role also is reinforced by this adventure launched for the sake of curing him, for he is now firmly convinced that knights do exist, that chivalric battles do occur, and that enchanters are still at work distorting reality even though sometimes they do so in unusual ways. Thomas Cecial is still able to choose, and he chooses to go home, cured of his folly, though he still addresses Sampson as "your worship." Sampson, however, now driven by revenge, becomes obsessed with knighthood for less generous reasons than Don Quixote's apparently altruistic ones. He has found an excellent excuse for continuing in his chivalric role; his previous alibi, to restore Don Quixote to his wits, was barely credible enough to carry the weight of his adventure. However, he now identifies completely with the part he plays. Carrasco is now a knight, not just a compliant neighbor dressing up to humor his friends.

Don Quixote, although extremely joyous at his victory, would doubtless have been better off had he, like Cecial, accepted his station in life for what it was. Is he really a "holy madman" (See W. H. Auden, *The Dyer's Hand*, p. 136) or only an impoverished landowner trying to compensate for his lowly station. The pathos of his quest stems partly from his self-deception about its causes. He learns to know himself only when it is too late.

* * *

In reading *Don Quixote* one cannot help but be constantly aware of the parallels and contrasts with *King Lear*. Both were written about the same time, both deal with madness (voluntary and involuntary), with pride, and with blindness to self. The heroes are men defrauded, one by self, the other by circumstances, of their rightful positions in society. The books concern the various ways in which they deal with their dilemmas. Cervantes' is the wider and larger vision; Shakespeare's the deeper. Shakespeare's concentration is chiefly on the hero and his counterpart in the sub-plot, the Duke of Gloucester. Cervantes' is on his hero and the world he meets. The wandering of Lear, though briefer, is more revealing psychologically; the wandering of Don Quixote raises more social and philosophical considerations. (Shakespeare was, of course, forced to work within a more rigid time structure because of the genre he employed, the play.)

Of particular interest in both works is the Renaissance concern with the human psyche and its outward manifestations. Both show that man behaves in strange ways because he does not understand himself. The actions of Lear and Quixote are self-defeating, for although both desire honor and esteem, neither knows the way in which to achieve it.

Chapter 16

As if to underline the blindness of Don Quixote to his own folly, Cervantes introduces us in this chapter to the Gentleman in Green, a man who is apparently not blind to himself, but actually, like Don Quixote, does not recognize his flaws. The measured good sense of Don Diego is ideal only for Don Diego himself. Cervantes is too great an artist to attempt to draw for us the portrait of "the perfect gentleman," and his book is no book of etiquette. Without the follies of Don Quixotes and Don Diegos, the world would be a dull place.

Moreover, one has to be somewhat suspicious of a man who proclaims his virtues so loudly to a stranger on the road. Don Diego tells us that he shares his goods with the poor without boasting, that he is no gossip, that he is a peacemaker. It is obvious that modesty is not among his list of virtues. Had Cervantes really wanted to portray the goodness of this man, should not his praise have come from others in the village? And when Sancho desires to do obeisance to him as a saint, he tells Sancho he is no saint but a sinner—jumping from one end of the scale to the other, from undue pride to undue humility.

We learn further that as a father he is rather overbearing, desiring his son to practice law or study theology and decrying his interest in poetry. With this point Don Quixote takes issue, defending poetry and the right of young people to choose their own vocations. So instead of Cervantes' ideal figure, the Gentleman in Green is in fact another foil for Don Quixote. Each possesses characteristics the other lacks; Don Quixote's imagination and Don Diego's practicality comment upon one another.

Don Quixote's disquisition on poetry is of considerable interest in itself. He attempts to show the Gentleman in Green that he is wrong to reject art as a career for his son, nor should his son be snobbish in judging Spanish poetry. One advantage of Don Quixote's position as anachronistic knight, outside the structure of his own society, is that he is not imbued with its taboos and its accepted standards. Therefore, his perspective is often clearer than that of those within the social fold.

But Don Quixote's acceptance of the imaginative arts as vocations gives us a clue to the purpose of his whole mission. As well as a justification of his own existence, his mission asserts the importance of fantasy and the world of the mind. For Cervantes recognizes that although the experiences of the body are limited by both time and space, the range of the mind is endless. Thus Don Quixote tells the Gentleman in Green that all other sciences serve and adorn poetry; he tries to show men how to live with their imaginations as well as with their bodies.

Chapter 17

Differences between Don Quixote and the Gentleman in Green are nowhere more clearly brought out than in the adventure with the lions. It is almost as if Don Quixote challenged the lions in order to emphasize Don Diego's deficiencies. In fact, he suggests that Don Diego should attend to his "quiet pointer" and "good ferret" (573) while he, Don Quixote, takes care of the cage of lions. Later in the chapter he speaks of the advantages of rashness over cowardice. The nucleus of the chapter is the definition of courage and that of madness. Don Diego, who has never mistaken a helmet full of curds for the softening of his brain and who has never braved hungry lions, is seen to be sane but rather staid. Don Quixote, who is mad, at least reaches for the extraordinary, for the miracle that man inwardly desires.

Two things differentiate this episode from earlier ones. First, Don Quixote is never mistaken as to the identity of the lions. He sees them for what they are and challenges them knowing the character of the danger he invites. Had the world of reality presented more adventures, perhaps Don Quixote would not have had to invent them, to make giants out of windmills. In one sense, then, it is the tame world of the Don Diegos which is at fault, of Don Diegos who tend their cabbage patches and perform their daily round of appointed duties. One is forced at times to be "mad" in order to shake the world by its shoulders and to set new courses for it. When real lions appear, Don Quixote does not have to invent them. Still, both the keeper and the Gentleman in Green see Don Quixote's actions as senseless; to let hungry lions out of their cages is to invite disaster.

The second difference between this episode and preceding ones is that the danger never materializes. The lion decides not to come out. Even real lions have lost the fierceness of lions in books of chivalry. (RIQ, 143) In previous episodes Don Quixote's luck was invariably bad. In this scene, he is easily able to make his point that even hungry lions may be subdued by the invincible spirit. It is the wisdom of all adventurers who have ever lived, and Don Diego does not miss the point, for at the end he invites Don Quixote to rest from his labors "of the spirit." Had the lion emerged, the book, of course, might well have ended with this chapter, and Don Diego would have returned to his home with the firm determination to guard his cabbage patch with even greater care. To open the door of the cage is perhaps foolhardy, but it is an option life gives to all of us. Our choice marks us as either Telemachus or Odysseus, the householder or the man for whom adventure is never done.

The Gentleman in Green is the first to point out that true courage does not consist of taking undue chances. But Cervantes himself, with his military career, his years of captivity involving attempted escapes, his service to the government of Spain, was one who accepted the risks of active living. Awaiting promotion at a small military post or later awaiting his freedom from captivity, Cervantes must often have wished for cages full of lions. Don Quixote's feat seems mad to Don Diego only because it has no apparent purpose. But Cervantes is showing us that a demonstration of the courage to face lions is an end in itself and worth almost any risk. For Don Diego "the better part of valour is discretion"; for Don Quixote one must accept risks and on occasion invite danger, even if in doing so one may appear rash or lacking in discretion.

Chapter 18

Don Diego and his son, Don Lorenzo, see Quixote as "mad in patches" and as "a brave madman." Don Lorenzo, however, who, despite Don Quixote's praise, is only a mediocre poet, could take many lessons from the knight. Don Quixote himself seems to see this and wishes he could take Lorenzo with him to teach him the accomplishments of the chivalric role. He needs breadth, understanding, and judgment to become a man of genius. A year with Don Quixote would enlighten him, would leave him no time for the composition of glosses which he writes to exercise his wits. But, like most of the persons Don Quixote meets, Don Diego and his son fail to see the reflections of their own folly in Don Quixote's mission. Don Quixote may be "a brave madman," but is he any madder than the man who spends his time writing glosses to exercise his wits? Don Quixote urges the youth to be guided by the opinion of others rather than by his own. For Don Lorenzo is basically a self-centered adolescent who could learn the virtues of knight-errantry from one who has practised them. Knight-errantry is, as Don Quixote points out, a narrow path, narrower even than poetry written to exercise the wits can be.

Chapter 19

In order to examine the question of forms even further, Cervantes gives us two more examples in this chapter. Although Don Lorenzo has served form too strictly, Cervantes does not leave us with the impression that he would do away with it entirely. For instance, Don Quixote speaks on the side of "arranged marriages," arguing that love may blind the understanding of a person and that "a safe and peaceful mate" is best on a long journey. (Yet, despite Don Quixote's talk, we find Basilio winning his love in a later chapter.) Doubtless Cervantes could see both sides of this subject. His own marriage at 37 to a girl with a small dowry, eighteen years his junior, had lasted only a few months. A year earlier another woman, Ana Franca de Rojas, had borne him a natural daughter.

The question of form also arises in the sword fight between the two students. Here there can be no question of the outcome. The licentiate with his superior technique is able to wear out the bachelor and to cut his clothes to shreds. Form and feeling both serve their own ends, and in poetry a blending of the two is surely necessary.

Chapter 20

The mock-heroic opening of this chapter sets the tone for the humorous juxtaposition of Don Quixote's romantic idealism and Sancho's earthiness which follows. Don Quixote has scarcely finished his elaborate address to the sleeping Sancho when with the butt end of his lance he awakens his squire, whose first thoughts are of food and whose next thoughts are of Camacho's money. In fact, the entire chapter seems to mock Don Quixote's opening speech on the "vain pomps of the world." (594) The ideal squire, who, according to Don Quixote, has no cares other than his ass, turns out, when awake, to have many more. The emphasis in the chapter is on the joys of this world—the dancers, the masque, and the food. In fact, Sancho puts away three hens and a couple of geese and terms them only "skimmings," and Cervantes notes that the huge cauldrons of food have been prepared by no less than fifty cooks. Sancho, enchanted by the opulence of Camacho, can see no virtue in the poverty-ridden Basilio. So intoxicated is he by the great feast that he sees even death as a "devourer" and declares that he who preaches well lives well. Throughout Sancho's eulogies Don Quixote is only mildly critical; the triumph of Basilio is to occur in the next chapter.

The Camacho-Basilio controversy is still another statement of the opposition of the real and the ideal. Sancho and Camacho dominate this chapter. The outer world of possessions is the world of Camacho's wedding. Camacho is buying Quiteria as he would buy a prize lamb. And Sancho, despite Don Quixote's gentle admonitions, feels that Camacho's is the best of all possible worlds. And yet, as the following chapter suggests, reality does not end with Sancho's skimmings, and Basilio turns out to have some virtues after all, despite his extreme poverty.

Chapter 21

In an earlier chapter (19) Sancho had defended Basilio's claim, and Don Quixote had spoken in favor of arranged marriages. Now the roles seem to have been reversed. Actually, however, in each instance Sancho and Don Quixote are true to their own visions of reality. Sancho's appreciation of the material side of life is the basis of his early defense of Basilio and his later intoxication with Camacho's food, while Don Quixote's idealism inspires his speech on arranged marriages and later his armed support of Basilio. It is impossible to judge either Sancho or Don Quixote by one isolated action; each action must be considered in relation to the total behavior pattern.

*   *   *

The mock heroic element is particularly noticeable in this section of the book. The opening of Chapter 21 has already been discussed. Now Don Quixote's defense of stratagem in love and war is a reminder of the Trojan horse, and his brandishing of his lance (so vigorously that it struck fear "into all who did not know him"), has a mock heroic ring. The epic hero, by contrast, struck fear into those who *did* know him. However, in defending Basilio, Don Quixote, despite his age and his angularity, is more of a knight than shining armor could ever make him. To strike fear into those who know one is perhaps as foolish as to strike fear into those who do not.

Basilio's trick itself adds to the mockery which pervades this chapter. It is a trick belonging to slapstick comedy, a contrivance which is barely convincing. Camacho, Quiteria, and Basilio are minor figures whom Cervantes uses to develop the plot, for Don Quixote's mission must encompass every facet of humanity. The point of the episode is not Basilio's trick, but Don Quixote's discernment in choosing between Camacho and Basilio and thus remaining true to his ideals. Sancho's mind, filled with materialistic concerns, cannot see beyond Camacho's lust, but Sancho does not need to see further, for Don Quixote sees for him. This is what Don Quixote meant when he referred to his "care of Sancho." (594)

Chapter 22

Don Quixote's idealism does not extend beyond the bounds of good sense when chivalry is not in question. He urges Basilio to amass some wealth, for love cannot live in poverty. In fact, he doubts that a poor man can be honorable, for then his wife, if she is beautiful, becomes the prey of all the crows and kites; great virtue is needed to repulse them. By "honorable" Don Quixote means, of course, "uncuckolded." And he is not so naive as to suppose that a "good" woman is necessarily good. He advises Basilio to consider reputation, for a woman is good if she appears to be so and a man honorable if he is not dishonored in public.

This clearly proves Don Quixote's ability to perceive the complexities of the practical world and what others see as reality. But it is necessary to remember that Don Quixote himself is single and harbors no thoughts of marriage. His love is for an ideal woman whom he has never seen. Thus his speech is theoretical in nature. His suspicions of women are particularly revealing. A good woman may only appear to be good. For Basilio and Quiteria all this talk is irrelevant anyway. Basilio has just won the girl he has loved since childhood. Cuckolding must seem a remote possibility at best. Don Quixote is like a man talking to the wind. His words are not of immediate importance in this particular situation any more than his defense of arranged marriages had been in Chapter 19.

Sancho, however, immediately puts the matter to the test by complaining of the "goodness" of his wife, Teresa, an example which discredits Don Quixote's argument, for it is obvious that it is neither Sancho's poverty nor Teresa's character which has caused trouble in this marriage, but rather a husband who absents himself for months on end. Don Quixote himself is then, at least indirectly, the cause of one cuckolding; the pursuit of knight-errantry as well as the condition of poverty may result in an unhappy marriage.

* * *

Following the wedding festivities comes the visit to Montesinos' cave (a mock-epic visit to the underworld). One of Cervantes' favorite devices is the juxtaposition of such opposites as a wedding and a visit to the underworld. The cave is introduced to the pair by a scholar, "by profession a humanist." (610) Cervantes' satire of Sampson Carrasco is mild in comparison with his satire of this scholar, possibly based on a real person, Francisco de Luque Faxardo, whose research concerns such details as discovering the first man to have catarrh; even Sancho recognizes the foolishness of the creature. Humanism, which, together with the finest accomplishments of the Renaissance, has encouraged all types of scholarly chicanery, is seen here in its worst light. Cervantes' satire is bitter against those who pervert scholarship to petty ends.

The descent into the cave, the flock of crows and daws which emerge, the mumbo-jumbo of Sancho's incantations (full of malapropisms), the slack rope, and Don Quixote's dream, all make this chapter one of the most hilarious in the book. No wonder the adventure is introduced by an empty-headed humanist, for on the surface it makes about as much sense as he does. Don Quixote has descended only thirty feet although 150 feet of rope have been paid out. The scholar has likewise delved very superficially into his area of research although he expends a great deal of energy. And like Don Quixote's acts, the scholar's books are unrelated to reality and incredible. Sancho will believe neither the scholar's words nor his master's dream.

The scholar and Don Quixote get along well together, for the scholar takes Don Quixote seriously, even his wildest pronouncements. Riquer suggests that the two were made for each other. In the scholar we find another mirror image of Don Quixote, "a Don Quixote of erudition." (RIQ, 144) Like Don Quixote's, his humanistic idealisms misfire and become the opposite of idealisms. Like the Don, he is often concerned with trivia. His *Book of Liveries* stresses, as the Don has stressed, the outer trappings of existence. Yet unlike Don Quixote, he does not descend into the cave. He does not, in other words, confront himself. He is content to stay on the surface rather than follow the more rigorous course of the knight.

For Don Quixote's descent into the cave, with all its parallels in literature and mythology (from the descents of classical heroes into Hades to the descent in *Las Sergas de Esplandín* which doubtless inspired Cervantes, RIQ, 144), symbolizes man's confrontation of his own inner world. It is this inner world which the scholar denies with his stress on detail and on outer form. The heroes of mythology and romance supposedly emerge from their underworlds with new insight or knowledge for the continuing of their quests. Don Quixote, in parody of these heroes, descends only thirty feet, falls asleep and dreams, and confronts a truth which he is not yet able to recognize fully. The scholar, however, fails even to descend and is thereby denied the possibility of ascent.

Chapter 23

Don Quixote's descent to the underworld consists chiefly of a dream he has while asleep on his ledge—a dream which reveals certain aspects of Don Quixote's own underworld, his subconscious. It can be seen, in a sense, as wish fulfillment, the dream of a knight's death as he would like it to be, attended by a loyal friend and lamented by countless lovely maidens led by the lady Belerma. It is the perfect death for a hero. It embodies the childish fantasy of watching one's own funeral rites, for Durandarte at times awakens and utters sighs and complaints. His heart is preserved apart from him by the lady Belerma. The dream also represents symbolically Don Quixote's actual condition, though he would not admit it. His heart, like Durandarte's, is cut from him and lies in the possession of the lady Dulcinea. No earthly love for woman can then threaten him. Both interpretations fit the underworld setting, for both center on death, death of the body and death of the heart.

In the dream Don Quixote finds Dulcinea "leaping and frisking" with two other peasant girls. The source here seems to be Don Quixote's meeting with the three peasant girls in Chapter 10 of this book, a scene deeply engraved in his mind, as frequent references to Dulcinea's enchantment show. Don Quixote's women tend to extremes; either they are exalted beauties or they are common sluts. There is no middle ground. It is clear from the dream that beneath his idealization of his lady lies a conviction that she is in reality exactly the opposite of his ideal, the girl he saw in the fields outside El Toboso. And as Gerald Brenan writes, Don Quixote knows unconsciously that "if any Dulcinea is ready to listen to his advances, it will be because she is mercenary." (COL, 26) Just as in his first stop at an inn in the 1605 *Quixote,* he mistakes prostitutes for "maidens," so he is just as capable of mistaking maidens for prostitutes. Rarely does he see a woman as a human being possessing both good and evil qualities, as his advice to Basilio in Chapter 22 has shown us. At the same time, although he may unconsciously suspect that Dulcinea is a slut, in recounting his dream he is apparently not aware of her grotesqueness. He seems to have accepted Sancho's lie of her enchantment as truth.

In his analysis of the incident of Montesinos' Cave, Edward Sarmiento suggests that the modern term for what occurred in the cave would be *fantasy* (in Cervantes' day *meditation* or *contemplation*.) The essential aspect of the scene is that through this fantasy Don Quixote is able to face truth for the first time. The various symbols of knighthood in the fantasy (a beautiful garden; a crystal castle; an elder, Montesinos, become a knight; the living corpse; a grieving lady) all point to the failures of Don Quixote. (SAR, 152) He has been unable to realize his dream, as the vision of Dulcinea "leaping and frisking" suggests. According to Sarmiento, he seems in this scene, to accept the impossibility of carrying out his quest and to recognize its flaw in his inability to exteriorize its symbols. Thus in telling of his vision he does not bother to comment on the ungainly Dulcinea. For he now senses that once an ideal becomes incarnate it is no longer an ideal.

That this scene represents a major turning point in the novel is not entirely convincing. The case rests on too slender evidence, for the fact that he does not bother to comment on Dulcinea's ugliness may be interpreted in several ways. As suggested above, he has undoubtedly accepted Sancho's lie of her enchantment and has thought it unnecessary to say more. In fact, he does in a way comment on Dulcinea's state, for in the dream Montesinos tells him that the girls are "enchanted ladies of quality" (621), which can hardly be seen as an acceptance of reality. Furthermore, Don Quixote's descent is a parody of the descents of heroes in the romances, in which beautiful maidens were observed and new insights gained. In the dream or fantasy there may indeed be a suggestion of his *unconscious* recognition of failure in the many symbols of knighthood with which it is filled, and after telling the dream he shows some signs of depression. But consciously he still does not capitulate. Soon after we find him attacking puppets with the same vigor with which he had engaged the windmills.

Montesinos' Cave is reminiscent of Plato's cave where we must view shadows *as if* they were realities and be content (see K, 294). The entire question of Dulcinea suggests the ultimate mystery of faith which is not resolved even after Don Quixote finally comes to his senses. For the whole point of the book is to suggest that there is no answer to this question, that the existence or non-existence of Dulcinea is relative to the beholder. Herman Melville once suggested that Dulcinea might be a surrogate for God.

*   *   *

In this chapter we also see the beginning of Sancho's enlightenment. He stops taking Don Quixote so literally, and with surprising bravado, challenges Don Quixote outright, for the first time daring him to beat or kill him if he desires. For Sancho is no longer afraid of his master, but sees him for what he is. Although he is willing to admit that enchantment may make an hour *seem* like three days, he totally refuses to accept the reality of Don Quixote's story. Unable to accept Don Quixote literally, he is unable to substitute the symbolic values which his master's quest represents, but resorts to a mystical explanation—that Merlin has stuffed Don Quixote's head full of lies. As he seems to other onlookers, Don Quixote now seems laughable to Sancho.

And Don Quixote's own spirit seems to be lagging. He has not seriously challenged Montesinos' disparagement of Dulcinea in his dream, and now he does not react strongly to Sancho's laughter. In the 1605 *Quixote* he would have struck Sancho for such behavior, as he had in the episode at the fulling mills.

Throughout the entire chapter the cousin-scholar is a tacit onlooker, interrupting once to question Don Quixote pedantically on the "unity of time" in his dream, for how, the scholar wonders, could Don Quixote have experienced so much in an hour. Even Sancho knows the answer to the scholar's question.

Chapter 24

Cervantes uses this chapter to provide a bridge between two episodes and to serve as a catchall for several random thoughts. We learned from Cide Hamete that Don Quixote on his death bed confessed that his dream was indeed invented. This fact in no way negates the interpretation of it given in the preceding pages. Nor does it justify Sancho's doubts. It merely reinforces Cervantes' point that literal-minded men have always viewed reality differently from men of imagination. Invention, rightly used, serves its own ends, although the reader is hard put to find a knightly virtue in the cave episode, unless it be the initial bravery necessary to begin the descent. Some courage is needed by all men who are prepared and willing to explore their own inner worlds. Although Don Quixote does not perceive the significance of his dream, and later retracts it, Cervantes may. However, Don Quixote does see in the following chapter (637) that his dream may be *both* imaginary and real.

The scholar, however, in his plodding way persists in distorting everything he views. For him the dream provides certain facts which will supply him with footnotes for his forthcoming books. When the matter of dedications for the scholar's books comes up, Cervantes slyly uses the opportunity to refer to "a prince who can supply the defects of all the rest" (625), a mocking comment on a system in which patrons are to be found for books such as those of this scholar.

*   *   *

Despite the episodic nature of the book, Cervantes rarely uses devices to create anticipation. However, in this chapter we meet an arms carrier, hurrying along the road and are promised his story later. Normally Cervantes will create anticipation simply by ending a chapter at the beginning or in the middle of an adventure, as with the battle with the Basque (1605) or the cave episode (1615). We see him experimenting with various fictional techniques which have since become standard ones.

* * *

Often overlooked in this chapter is Cervantes' jab at hermits. The hermit in this chapter, despite his religious commitments, has provided himself with the comforts of home and a so-called "under-hermitess" (626). It would seem he does not live in the strictest of solitudes.

* * *

The final section of the chapter, concerning the lad on the way to war, provides Don Quixote with the opportunity to expatiate on a favorite subject, arms and letters. As usual he defends arms as winning more honor than letters and urges the boy to forget all possible disasters, for death is the ultimate disaster. Don Quixote is articulate, and his talk is not unrelated to his actions, even though the latter often misfire and make his talk seem empty. Perhaps his weakness is his strength, for had he been a younger man, he doubtless would have long since become a target for the military or civil authorities. It is his relative harmlessness which saves him and enables him to retain the attention and concern of his audience.

Chapter 25

Cervantes' talent for comedy is superbly illustrated in the episode describing the braying of the alderman and his friend, another alderman. Each man takes the other's braying with perfect seriousness, complimenting him on the realism of his performance. At the beginning, until the signals are set up, they mistake each other for the ass. The conclusions are all too evident. But the arguments and fights which ensue from this harmless search are far from harmless. Stupid as the aldermen may be, they at least find the dead ass. The aldermen have a constructive purpose; the warring villagers, however, act from a sense of false pride and the only result of their action is a few broken bones. Cervantes never tires of showing us that what may seem foolish on the surface is often far less foolish than the reaction to it.

Before the outcome of the fight is known, we are introduced to Master Peter and his prophesying ape. The various kinds of actors met on the way are of particular interest because they serve as foils for Don Quixote. Cervantes himself traveled for a time with a company of actors; furthermore, much of his youth was spent traveling with his family (for his father was an itinerant dealer in medicines, following the route of the country fairs.) Master Peter is, of course, a fake; but both Don Quixote and Sancho are fooled by the prophesying ape. Don Quixote, thinking that the ape must have made some pact with the devil, wonders why the Inquisitor does not examine him. Actually, however, the ape is as harmless as Don Quixote. Peter is the one who poses the danger. Not only does he earn his living by trading on other people's credulities, turning them into apes like his own, but he is a criminal wanted by the civil authorities. Unlike Don Quixote, Master Peter has no high aims and no goal other than to escape his punishment and to extort a living from others by almost any means. The aldermen have just been equated with asses; now an actor is found in the company of an ape. Master Peter is, in fact, only aping an actor, and he is living on borrowed time. Don Quixote, by comparison, is not just aping a knight; he is one.

Chapter 26

The puppet show, like many other elements of *Don Quixote* —the digressive essays, the vision in the cave, the tales—is another play within a play which comments on the main theme of the book. The subject of the show, the rescuing of Melisendra by her husband, Sir Gaiferos, reflects Don Quixote's mad fantasies of protecting maidens in distress so closely that Don Quixote confuses the play with reality. The melodrama of the show is the melodrama of Don Quixote's mind. He himself would be Sir Gaiferous with whom he readily identifies. Yet the venture of Sir Gaiferous, who is removed from fleshly existence by both fiction and pasteboard, is, in a way, more "practical" than that of Don Quixote: the Don is bent on destroying another's property, while Sir Gaiferous, is occupied in regaining his own. Yet Don Quixote does come to see his error and pays for it willingly, having made his point to his own satisfaction, if not to Sancho's and that of the other people present. We find here another example of Don Quixote's growing insight into his own behavior.

Truth all depends on perspective. As Don Quixote declares, it is "right to help fugitives." (643) But no sooner do we admit this and judge him far superior to Master Peter than we remember that it was he who freed Master Peter, enabling him to continue his criminal career. Don Quixote makes no distinction between fugitives from justice and fugitives from injustice. He has helped Sir Gaiferous in his justifiable flight from the Moor, and Gines (Master Peter) in his escape from captivity with the galley slaves (Chapter 27-1605). Are all fugitives to be helped to escape simply because they are fugitives? The chapter opens some grave issues about the nature of Don Quixote's quest. There are various ways of helping the unfortunate, and Don Quixote does not always suit the means to the end. But he is lovable because he makes mistakes, because he is like all of us, something less than the "perfect knight." Cervantes' genius rests in his having created

an ambiguous and multi-dimensional character, a human being
no more or less mad than mankind as a whole. We tend to
idealize Don Quixote because as the book progresses we identify
with him and take his side. Yet Cervantes would show us a man
with all the complexities of a human being. Although Don
Quixote can never be the perfect knight, we love him because
he at least aspires to be one. The purposes of Cervantes and his
hero are strangely similar. Each asserts a fiction in order to
attain a higher end. Don Quixote fails because his fiction has no
real basis in the physical world, whereas Cervantes succeeds because he turns Don Quixote's fiction into a reality, the reality of
art. Arms and letters both have a function of their own, as Don
Quixote never tires of telling us. In both military and literary
worlds, imagination is an indispensable quality, but it must be
effective, which Don Quixote's ventures too often are not. It is
through Cervantes that Don Quixote triumphs at the end.

Chapter 27

We leave Master Peter and his ape in "peace and amity"
to return to the braying villagers. It is not simple chance that
apes and asses are introduced in quick succession as counterparts
of man. Cervantes' wit is both subtle and biting.

Don Quixote's advice to the army of villagers is reasonable,
but quite inconsistent with his own folly. True, no individual can
insult a whole village, and true, one should take up arms only for
just causes. Don Quixote's blindness to his own folly is never
more evident than in this speech. Whoever takes up arms "for
matters laughable and amusing" is "lacking in all common sense,"
Don Quixote tells us (650). In his own judgment Don Quixote
does not take up arms for such purposes. The matters become
laughable and amusing only because other people think them so.
But neither do the villagers deem their purpose to be laughable
and amusing. They are in dead earnest to avenge an insult. Essen-

tially, however, the purpose of the villagers differs from that of Don Quixote, for they are interested solely in reestablishing a reputation which has never been seriously threatened to begin with. Furthermore, it is not the principle of honor which matters to them but the insult itself. A sense of humor could have solved the whole affair. Don Quixote's adventures often turn out to be about as empty as this venture of the brayers, but they are not inspired by shoddy ideals. The villagers have no real rationale behind their action, as Don Quixote vainly tries to point out to them. They represent a position opposite Don Quixote's, for they have the practical means to put their foolish plans into action whereas Don Quixote has high-minded plans without the practical means to implement them. His behavior is at complete variance with his ideas of what behavior should be. In one sense, he is a child playing soldier; in another, he maintains ideals which surpass those of most adults. For Don Quixote the boundary between fact and fantasy is often practically obscured.

Sancho, however, makes mincemeat of Don Quixote's words of wisdom to the brayers. No sooner does Sancho begin to bray than the villagers take offense, and Don Quixote is forced to flee. As has been suggested, the 1615 *Quixote* shows Don Quixote's growing awareness of the nature of the world around him. In the 1605 book, flight would never have been an alternative for the knight.

Furthermore, Sancho's words and actions, not Don Quixote's, are the ones that spark this episode. Earlier, Sancho was always the one to urge retreat and to leave well enough alone. Sancho's new bravado, seen first at the cave of Montesinos, leads to catastrophe in this chapter, for he is beaten black and blue. The "practical" Sancho is no more practical here than Don Quixote is "idealistic." Labels are deceptive, Cervantes shows us. Sancho fails here for the very reason that his master so often fails, because his means of putting his idea into action are unfeasible. As Don Quixote later asks him (652), why show a rope to a hanged man's family?

Chapter 28

But judgments are easily made after an event has taken place, and Don Quixote himself has been as guilty as Sancho of the rashness of which he accuses his squire. Furthermore, his advice that "the better part of valor is discretion" sounds suspiciously like the advice of the Gentleman in Green in the episode of the lions. Retreat may not be flight, but to claim that he "retired" rather than "fled" is merely to rationalize.

It is at this point that Sancho, aching in every joint, begins to take stock. He wonders if such a venture is worth the pain it involves and whether or not he should return home. But Don Quixote, in one of his better moments, anticipating twentieth-century therapy, urges his squire to "talk things out." "Say everything that comes into your mind and into your mouth, my son, for if it relieves you of your pain I will willingly control the vexation your impertinences cause me." (653) Sancho at once turns to the subject nearest his heart—material benefits—his wages and his island. Whereas he had failed in his dealings with the brayers, he is now almost successful in dealing with Don Quixote about his wages.

But he becomes so greedy, demanding wages for the twenty years since Don Quixote promised him his isle, that his master first laughs and then becomes angry, telling him to go back home. This is one of the crucial moments of the 1615 *Quixote,* marking a near split between the pair. Don Quixote's wrath is kindled when he thinks of the contrast between Sancho and the squires of knights-errant in the books he has read. It is true that the contrast is stark, that Sancho has hardly filled his role of squire. Don Quixote, however, at the same time that he is telling Sancho to leave him is consciously or unconsciously giving Sancho two irresistible reasons for staying. First, since he has been such a poor squire, he should remain to work out his "indebtedness." Second, it is asinine to leave just as one is about to be established as governor of an isle. Thus Don Quixote, while saying the opposite, is actually arguing for Sancho to remain with him. Sancho's repentance is immediate when he hears Don Quixote's second reason, and he is all too ready to acknowledge himself an ass for the sake of becoming a governor. At the same time, Sancho's tears express a genuine remorse for his greedy behavior.

The significance of this episode is enhanced by its contrast with the section dealing with the pranks of the Duke and the Duchess which begins two chapters later. For one becomes aware here of the close ties of affection between Sancho and the Don, an affection which enables Don Quixote to accept an "ass" for a squire and which enables Sancho to "work" without wages for a madman. Each accepts flaws in the other, in fact loves the other despite his flaws. By contrast, the pranks of the Duke and Duchess are based on a mockery of human frailty, Don Quixote's madness and Sancho's credulity.

Chapter 29

However, in the adventure of the enchanted boat (a parody of knights who drifted in abandoned boats without guidance), Don Quixote and Sancho return to their customary roles. Now Don Quixote instigates the action and Sancho counsels caution. Nevertheless, both are drawn together into the mill-race. As in the puppet episode, Don Quixote is a madman, mistaking illusion for reality, and although he pays for the damage he has done he does not really awaken, since he persists in his fantasy and lays his failure to free his fellow knight to the enchanters. Even Cervantes seems for a moment to tire of the antics of his hero when he refers to his existence as "beast-like" (661). To establish Don Quixote's knighthood, more is needed than enchanted boats, and his worthy desire to assist a fellow knight is obscured by his blind actions to achieve that end. The lice-infested Sancho and the drenched knight return to the shore, seeming more like animals than human beings. In the 1615 *Quixote* animal imagery is of great importance. The lions, the ape, the asses, and later the bulls and the pigs which trample Don Quixote are used to make subtle points about the human race. In the episode of the enchanted boat Don Quixote and Sancho are reduced to the level of beasts. But at least Don Quixote has chosen his own course, whereas in the coming chapters he and Sancho become like the caged lions of Chapter 17.

The mill-race into which the pair are drawn in this episode represents loss of control. Until now they have moved on foot or on horseback, methods they can govern fairly readily. Here, however, lacking oar or rudder, they are swept on by the current; symbolically they lose the power of direction. This chapter fittingly precedes the episode with the Duke and the Duchess in which their adventure is directed by human forces for selfish ends. At least for Don Quixote, the new order of things after the ride in the enchanted boat turns out to be a prison of the spirit.

Chapter 30

In the next twenty-seven chapters we are involved in what becomes the longest "episode" of the entire book—the encounter with the Duke and Duchess, probably modeled on Don Carlos de Boya and Doña Maria de Aragon, who had a castle in Pedrola. (RIQ, 149) The nature of this episode differs markedly from all the others. As Cervantes has forecast in the previous chapter, the reins are now removed from Don Quixote's hands, and he and Sancho become pawns for the amusement of the "sophisticated" nobility. What happens to them is governed by the whims of the Duke and his spouse. And since they are not entirely aware of what is happening to them, Don Quixote and Sancho lose the dignity belonging to human beings. They begin to resemble animals kept in a cage or court jesters who are encouraged to behave in a foolish manner. The pathos of their plight is increased by

their guillibility. Unlike the priest, the barber, and Sampson
Carrasco, the Duke and Duchess do not have even the excuse of
trying to cure Don Quixote. They encourage his follies for their
own pleasure. To make one's fellow man the butt of one's practical jokes, especially a fellow man given to mad fantasies, is to
prove oneself lower than the fools which Don Quixote and
Sancho become. For these reasons this section of the book often
has an unsavory flavor, and the previous amusement of the reader
turns to distaste. It is as if the Duke and the Duchess assume
the prerogative of the gods. The whims of fate to which Don
Quixote and Sancho have been subjected are laughable because
all men are subject to them. Most men (whether literally or
figuratively) have found themselves at one time or another headed
for a mill-race in an open boat. But all men are not subject to
manipulation by other men, especially without being aware of it.
The Duke and the Duchess assume the role of Big Brother, and
we feel for them the same distaste that we feel for Orwell's figure.

Even fate seems ready to play the game of the Duke and
Duchess, for in dismounting to greet their hosts, Don Quixote
and Sancho become so entangled in their harnesses that help must
be ordered by the Duke. In fact, it is a wonder that the pair have
not long since been exploited by some entrepreneur, for they
have repeatedly presented the opportunity for such manipula-
tions. Sampson Carrasco was one of the few who may have been
tempted to "use" Don Quixote and Sancho, but he soon became
a convert, and after his defeat was as dead in earnest as Don
Quixote himself.

Yet P. E. Russell shows that the modern reader's reaction
to the crude pranks of the Duke and Duchess was not the reaction
of the Renaissance reader, who regarded any deviation from the
natural order of things with a sense of wonder and amusement.
(RUS, 320). For the reader of the seventeenth century these
chapters would not have been distasteful or lacking in propriety
but "funny." There is no reason, Russell concludes, to suggest
that Cervantes saw his work as anything but pure comedy. Although this last point may be overstated, it is important to remember that the perspectives of epochs as well as of people vary.
For if *Don Quixote* teaches us any lesson, it is the lesson of

understanding for others who may stand at vantage points different from our own.

Chapter 31

Cervantes' irony is never more pointed than in Don Quixote's remark, on entering the courtyard of the Duke and Duchess, that this is the first time he has been "positively certain" of being a true knight-errant. In addition to the mocking attitudes of the Duke and Duchess, Sancho unwittingly mocks his master with his foolish utterances and his argument with Doña Rodriguez. Once he discovers that he is fully "appreciated" by the Duchess and has her support, he is ready to amuse her even at his master's expense. His tale of the gentleman and the farmer openly discredits Don Quixote, and his description of Dulcinea, as nimble as a cat, pays less than homage to the lady of a knight. Don Quixote's stay at the castle is a kind of unwitting martyrdom in which all, even his squire, turn against him in mockery. Although, physically speaking, the pair have never been more comfortable they have never been at a lower ebb in the metaphysical sense, having lost sight of those values—dignity, courage, compassion, service—about which Don Quixote is fond of preaching. Tragically he is not and cannot be aware of what is happening to him, particularly at the beginning of his stay, for if ever there were a time for him to take arms, it is now, against the mockery of the Duke.

Another main theme of this chapter concerns the priest who lives at the castle. Cervantes takes this opportunity to satirize ecclesiastics who spend their time in the easy service of the rich. He even digresses briefly to generalize about priests who do not succeed in teaching their princes how to behave, who posssess a certain narrowness of soul, and who breed miserliness rather than frugality. The priest's anger at Sancho's prolixity is particularly amusing because it is evident that the priest has the same fault, as is suggested by the laughter of the Duke and Duchess. Further-more, the priest takes a firm stand against all tales of knight-errantry (he has long urged his master to abandon the reading of such nonsense). To stand face to face with Don Quixote, indeed to find himself in competition for the Duke's favor with a knight (for even ecclesiastics suffer the pangs of jealousy), is almost too difficult for the priest to bear, and he advises Don Quixote, in no uncertain terms, to go home and attend to his lands and children "if you have any" (673).

Chapter 32

Don Quixote's first line of defense against the priest's attack is "arms." He accuses the priest of using a woman's weapon, the tongue, rather than his own more manly weapons, the sword and the lance. Throughout his reply he stresses the unmanly qualities of the priest. Furthermore, he feels the priest is provincial since the latter knows only his own small district, while he has taken the world for his province. It appears that Don Quixote's tongue does not lag far behind his opponent's. His own course, by com-parison with the priest's, seems to him to be noble.

After Sancho is offered his island by the Duke, the priest is able to bear his position no longer; he retreats to his home, de-termined to remain there as long as the pair shall be at the castle. It is doubtless a wise move, for Don Quixote immediately ration-alizes that although his opponent may have been "offended," the priest, like women and children, is incapable of giving an "af-front." The name-calling might have grown beyond control had the priest remained at the castle. The priest and Doña Rodriguez are the only two persons not ordered by the Duke to treat Don Quixote as a Knight. So a sense of being excluded from a joke as well as a sense of jealousy may motivate the priest's anger and his retirement to his home. Don Quixote, the butt of the joke, endures.

The soaping of Don Quixote which follows is no less an insult than the attack by the priest. Moreover, it is abetted by the Duke, who orders a soaping for his own beard so that the prank of the maids will not be perceived. It is also more insidious than the attack by the priest, for Don Quixote is deluded into thinking it a courtesy of the country. To make Don Quixote look ludicrous is, of course, the only purpose of the maids.

Insult follows injury as the Duke urges Don Quixote to describe the peerless Dulcinea, intending to enjoy the knight's mad fantasies. After Don Quixote has mentioned Dulcinea's enchantment, the Duchess hints that Dulcinea may not exist at all, hoping to pique Don Quixote into an outburst of indignation. Instead the knight parries with the argument that only God knows whether she exists or not. Her ideal form is Don Quixote's concern, and the Duchess is thwarted. Next the Duke attempts to prod the knight by claiming that Dulcinea's lineage surely cannot compare with that of the Orianas. Since the Duke has read the 1605 *Quixote,* he expects such an attack on Dulcinea to produce a strong reaction. But Don Quixote, awed, it seems, by his surroundings, replies quite reasonably that works and virtues are more important than lineage. (It has been noted earlier that when Don Quixote feels that he is succeeding in his quest, his madness becomes less evident. In the false security and comfort of the castle, he seems temporarily and ironically to have achieved some balance and perspective.) The Duchess also launches an attack on Dulcinea's lineage, which she doubts because of the red wheat Dulcinea was said to be winnowing. Don Quixote is now forced to fall back on the enchanters—his convenient explanation for everything he cannot understand and his easy escape from reality. The patience of the Duke and Duchess is at last rewarded.

Even more droll to the ducal pair is the interruption from an enraged Sancho, who has been threatened in the kitchen with a washing in dirty water and lye. Don Quixote has just finished expressing great confidence in Sancho's skill at governing. Sancho now provides the hilarity, and in doing so he unwittingly blurts out the truth about the soapings—that they were more practical jokes than civilities.

Chapter 33

Criticism of *Don Quixote* often assumes that Don Quixote and Sancho interact upon one another and that by the end of the book each has absorbed qualities from the other and each emerges with a modified personality. This is true to some extent, but more so for Don Quixote than for Sancho. Sancho does not begin to believe in Don Quixote's fantasy of an enchanted Dulcinea until the Duchess tells him that *she* believes it. Sancho does not here assume Don Quixote's point of view, for his faith is still in things of this world—the Duchess's word—which he believes because of her status and wealth. He has to have a material reason for his faith; Don Quixote does not. Later (in Chapter 41) when Sancho tells the assembled company what he saw when he peeked through one corner of his blindfold on his trip into the sky on Clavileño, it does not mean that he has acquired his master's madness. He is simply playing the same sort of game he was playing when he enchanted Dulcinea, a game which the Duchess fails to perceive when she chides him for making the earth the size of a mustard seed and men the size of hazel nuts. Sancho, a peasant of the soil, could never have made this mistake unintentionally. In fact, Sancho has not left the earth and he knows it. The joke is on the Duchess. Sancho remains on solid ground.

However, it is necessary that the Duke and Duchess *think* that Sancho is deceived in order that they may enjoy their practical jokes. A knowing Sancho might alert Don Quixote. The Duchess believes she has convinced Sancho of the reality of enchanters and that he will play the game and cooperate, especially since his governorship depends partly on his belief.

The question of what constitutes reality is, once again, the central issue. Aldonza Lorenzo, not Dulcinea, exists in flesh and blood. But Sancho's "ideals" stretch just as far as money will take them, for he idealizes even the Duchess as a symbol of power and wealth. Don Quixote, on the other hand, idealizes Dulcinea as a symbol of exalted virtue. Reality, in the physical world, may be distorted either by love of money or by an idealism which transcends the physical. Yet repeatedly Sancho is saved from a purely physical existence through his faithful devotion to his master.

Chapter 34

The fine balance between truth and illusion continues in this chapter. The boar and its death and Sancho's predicament in the oak are all in the realm of fact. The Devil, who enters swearing by God and his conscience, is part of the Duke's pretense. But even the boar hunt is shown by Sancho to be as empty of meaning as the act which follows it. In fact, the Duke can give no real answer when Sancho asks why hunting should be a pleasure, "for it consists of killing an animal which has not committed any offence." (695) The Duke defends hunting as a discipline, as preparation and practice for war. Animals are to be sacrificed in the interests of war between men. Sancho with his love for Dapple cannot understand such reasoning. But Sancho's fear of the boar has to be kept in mind, for his sentiments on hunting surely spring partly from this fear. For Cervantes and the people of his time, Sancho's argument on hunting doubtless had little validity.

The lavish performance which follows shows the length to which the Duke and Duchess will go to satisfy their craving for the exotic. It also illustrates the aimless sort of activity which occupies the sophisticated and the wealthy. Cartloads of demons and sages, woods full of fireworks, the very Devil himself are provided by the Duke. Sancho's fears are once more aroused but now for a different reason—fear of the supernatural. For help he runs to the Duchess's skirts instead of to another oak tree. Both boar and demon have terrorized the simple peasant, who has neither the means to combat the boar nor the knowledge to dispel the demon. But what Sancho perceives, that killing an innocent animal can be no pleasure, far surpasses in compassion and humanity any sentiment expressed by the Duke either here or elsewhere. By comparison with the squire of a knight-errant, the Duke is a sham. At least Sancho's fear is a real fear, and his predicament in the oak tree a real, and not pretended, predicament. In the same way Don Quixote's fantasy of knight-errantry far surpasses the Duke's extravaganza; one is done for idle amusement, the other for a lofty purpose. Cervantes creates the Duke and Duchess, as he has created other figures, as foils for Don Quixote. Is the man who mistakes inns for castles more foolish than the idle exploiter of a madman? The hunt of the innocent boar is in a sense symbolic of the hunt the Duke and the Duchess are conducting for their amusement at the expense of Don Quixote. Sancho's fears, if not Don Quixote's, surely stem partly from his awareness of being the object of the ducal hunt.

Chapter 35

Sancho does in fact become the object of this hunt when Merlin approaches in his triumphal car and decrees (in the style of diabolical figures of the Middle Ages, RIQ, 152) that in order to disenchant Dulcinea Sancho must deal himself 3,300 lashes. The Duke and the Duchess "assume an appearance of fear" (699), but Sancho and Don Quixote tremble in reality. Moreover, Dulcinea is parodied by a youth dressed as a girl. Don Quixote, faced with insults to both his squire and his beloved, is unmoved. Instead of mounting and bearing arms against the enemy, Don Quixote threatens Sancho, his friend, with a double ration of lashes; nor is he able to see through the disguise worn by the lad posing as Dulcinea. When Sancho accepts the assignment to disenchant Dulcinea, under threat of losing his governorship, the Duke and the Duchess have succeeded in turning the knight's own fiction against his squire. Yet Sancho's common sense in administering the 3,300 lashes will save him. Furthermore, he now has a weapon to use against his master, who must beg or pay his servant to whip himself. Since Sancho enchanted Dulcinea, it is, of course, poetic justice that he should disenchant her.

Cervantes shows us in this episode that each man must come to his own defense as well as recognize who his real enemies are. Don Quixote has repeatedly attacked the innocent (sheep, puppets, the Basque) and spared the guilty (galley slaves, Master Peter, the Duke and Duchess). Now, when he is faced with a major threat of real proportion, he blindly ignores it and tragically misjudges the situation. Valor without the ability to apply that valor with insight is as useless as insight coupled with cowardice, Cervantes seems to be saying.

Chapter 36

This chapter serves as a transition between the episode of the disenchantment and that of the afflicted waiting woman. Sancho's letter to his wife describing the events of the past few days ties in with the preceding episodes, whereas the appearance of Trifaldin foreshadows what is to come. In his letter Sancho describes his master as "a sane madman and a droll idiot" (707). Such ambiguities are typical of Cervantes' subtle methods in handling character. Don Quixote may be an idiot to go to the assistance of a sham Countess; he may even be a madman to agree to Sancho's whipping. But the sanity of his intentions can never be questioned, whereas the sanity of the intentions of the Duchess, who provides Sancho with his whip, and of the steward, who arranges the affair of the afflicted waiting woman, can readily be doubted. Both the steward and the Duchess appear to be playing children's games.

It is curious that in a large number of the episodes at the castle the spotlight falls on Sancho rather than on Don Quixote. In fact, Don Quixote seems often to fade into the background here, allowing himself to be manipulated by others, whereas Sancho, encouraged by the Duchess's attentions and the promise of his governorship, takes on a new bravado. On one level of consciousness Don Quixote seems to be partially aware of the Duke's hoax; if he does not resist it, it is because he cannot. The world and its folly have saddened him into silence. On the other hand, his answer to Trifaldin's request that he grant audience to the Countess Trifaldi seems to indicate a reinforcement of his madness. He even wishes the skeptical priest were present to hear Trifaldin and to judge thereby the importance of knights-errant. In these ways he fulfills Sancho's description of him as a "sane madman."

Chapter 37

We continue to mark time in this chapter as we anticipate the appearance of the afflicted waiting woman. The delay produces an effect of satire, for such delays are usually connected with royalty or important persons. The Countess Trifaldi is, of course, only one of the Duke's servants in disguise.

Furthermore, the approach of the afflicted waiting woman revives temporarily the feud between Sancho and Doña Rodriguez. Waiting women and squires are commonly enemies, for they curry favor with the same masters and mistresses, and each stands in the same relation to nobility. Jealousy occurs among equals. If the Countess Trifaldi suffers the affliction of a beard, Doña Rodriguez suffers from a different kind of affliction, one named Sancho, who terms all waiting women "meddlers and troublemakers." (711) We still await the appearance of the Countess.

Chapter 38

The satire begun by the delaying tactics in the two preceding chapters continues with the description of the entrance of the Countess. Her proper title, Benengeli tells us, is the Countess of Wolves. Riquer points out that through the Countess's titles (Trifaldi suggesting the three banners of the house of Osuna which resembled the coats-of-arms of Lobuna and Zorruna), Cervantes may maliciously allude to the writer Luis Gálvez de Montalvo and Magdalena Girón. (OB, 868)

On the other hand, Leo Spitzer has a further explanation. (SP, 48-49) He suggests that Cervantes' etymological 'mistake' in explaining *Trifaldi* as meaning literally *three skirts* is a conscious parody of medieval etymology. The real source of both *Trifaldin* and *Trifaldi* is the Italian *Truffaldino* (the name of a low and ridiculous character in comedy). Furthermore, the names may also be related to the verb, *truffare,* to cheat, since the purpose of both characters is to deceive Don Quixote and Sancho. The whole basic question of appearance and reality is thus underlined even in the etymological constructions in the book.

It is Sancho, with his dislike of waiting women, who replies to her in elaborate mockery of the lady's diction. But the mockery is perhaps the result of another element—Sancho's awe before regal ceremony. It is not entirely clear whether his purpose is to mock the lady or to show off his own prowess in courtly language. Since, however, we know Sancho's feelings about waiting women, we can probably assume that his attitude toward the Countess is basically cynical. Cervantes' purpose, of course, is evident—to ridicule all sham and pretense; thus, Sancho's speech, whether spoken in mockery or not, shows us the silly nature of ladies-in-waiting.

Don Quixote, on the contrary, replies to the lady in all seriousness. As a knight-errant he should, of course, have had insight into the drama unfolding before him. But his confusion of the trappings of his role with its mission leads him again and again into the dilemma of offering his protection to a charlatan, here a disguised waiting man acting for the idle amusement of his lord and lady.

Once the waiting woman begins her tale, the mockery increases. The tale consists of an elaborate sentimental romance; the language used is obviously masculine rather than feminine. At the end of the chapter the reader is left in suspense with the upshot of the seductions by Don Clavijo of both the princess and the waiting woman still in doubt. But the interest created is so artificial that the suspense in itself is hardly more than mockery.

Chapter 39

The satisfaction of the reader's curiosity about the Countess's story must wait until Sancho has had his word. A skeptic at heart, he interrupts to ask if, when the princess's mother was buried, she was dead, and to suggest that she would have done better to faint rather than die. Sancho doubtless could improve on the Countess's story—for in his opinion it is hardly realistic. Sancho's doubt again reflects his attitude toward waiting women as well as a growing sophistication. He is now able to pass judgment on the drama of which he is a part rather than to accept it at face value. Cervantes uses these interpositions partly to remind us that we are still in the court of the Duke and Duchess and that the story must be judged in relation to its listeners. The point of view of the Countess, which is based on fantasy, must be compared with that of Sancho, whose feet are planted on the ground. But although Sancho's criticism of the story is reassuring by comparison with Don Quixote's passive acceptance of it, Sancho is perhaps as pathetic as his master, for he can see no farther than the farce which is being played, and continually directs his criticism at the wrong things and people for the wrong reasons. Thus the servant who plays the waiting woman (as well as the Duke and Duchess) should be the butt of Sancho's anger, and the story deserves criticism not for its lack of reality, but because its purpose is both frivolous and cruel.

The giant who turns the lovers into a crocodile and a brass monkey adds to the inflated character of this tale. Once the veils of the Countess and her servants are removed and the "bearded women" discovered, the scene becomes grotesque. Sancho and Don Quixote have entered a world of nightmares, and our pity at their acceptance of the delusion is exceeded only by our contempt for the Duke, the Duchess and their staff.

Chapter 40

However, Sancho and Don Quixote are not simply the butt of the humor in these scenes, but in a way recognize that what is happening is a game although the Duke and Duchess do not realize this. So, in a sense, the tables are turned, and it is the Duke and Duchess who are being fooled without realizing it, for without the cooperation of the pair, they could not proceed. Sancho, in particular, is conscious of his role; his reluctance to mount Clavileño is in part sheer play, as is Trifaldi's speech in which she recounts names *not* belonging to Clavileño. Both Sancho and Trifaldi are enjoying their roles as much as their audiences are. " 'How many, now, does this horse take?' asked Sancho." (723)

The mock epic element in this chapter is, of course, evident, in the inventions of the Duke's servants. Clavileño is an obvious descendant of Pegasus as well as of the wooden horse of Troy. The list given by Trifaldi of all the horses he is not, like Bucephalus and Orelia, mocks epic stylistics. Like Pegasus, Clavileño flies, and like the wooden horse of Troy, he is stuffed with "firecrackers." Cervantes shows us that even the servants of a Duke and Duchess can "invent" wooden horses filled with "warriors." As Riquer states, flying horses had been present in chivalric tales for more than three centuries, having perhaps originated in one

of the tales of *A Thousand and One Nights,* and Spanish readers
were well-acquainted with various versions of the flying horse
theme and would have recognized the parody (RIQ, 153).

Chapter 41

The adventure of the afflicted waiting woman is perhaps too
long and too detailed. Sancho's recognition of the hoax is now
perfectly evident. But since the world of the Duke and Duchess
is an upside-down one, Sancho feels justified in creating his own
distorted world. He continues to invent in great detail the phenomena of his flight on Clavileño, who came burning down
through the air. The inventions of Sancho parallel Don Quixote's
inventions at the Cave of Montesinos, and master and squire
strike a bargain to believe one another's stories, a tacit recognition
by both that the "play" is what matters. In other words, although
the man behind the mask is related to the character he plays, he
is not that character. Cervantes recognizes that all men wear
masks. We project our purposes and intentions in life by means
of roles. Organized society is a kind of theater where man
chooses a part to play either to promote or to destroy that society.
In a way, Sancho and Don Quixote are more conscious of the
nature of their roles than the Duke and Duchess, who believe
themselves to be the benevolent and fun-loving owners of a large
and noble estate, while they are actually two frivolous and sometimes cruel people, who will stop at nothing, even the ridicule of
a mad man, for their pleasure. Sancho, however, is perfectly aware
that, despite his title of squire, his real role is as a friend to his
master, and Don Quixote knows that the designation of knight
carries with it a duty to serve and to love the helpless and the
afflicted, whom the Duke and Duchess have parodied in the guise
of the "afflicted" waiting woman. The Duke is noble in name
only; Don Quixote is noble in spirit. The destruction caused by
Don Quixote is in the physical realm (puppets or a boat, things

easily replaced.) The Duke, however, with his jokes, unwittingly aims at the very heart of Don Quixote's high-minded enterprise.

Chapter 42

Sancho's ardor for a governorship has partially cooled since the hoax of Clavileño. In fact, he reasons almost out loud that if the flight into the sky has been a joke, this governorship must be an even worse one. Sancho is gaining more and more perspective. If the world is a mustard seed, what is the glory in governing it? But despite his new insights, he is still naive enough to agree to accept the governorship and to imagine that money, position, and title by themselves bring satisfactions. The Duke's advice to Sancho is in sharp contrast to Don Quixote's, for the sweetest thing, according to the Duke, is to give orders and to be obeyed. Don Quixote, on the other hand, recognizes office as "a deep gulf of confusion" (737). The Duke's superficiality in regard to the business of life is clear here, for he turns everything, even the serious matter of leadership, into a joke.

The whole question of governing had taken on a new light with the advent of the Renaissance. For the first time, the ruler was seen as a human being, subject to the same errors of judgment as other men. Books flourished on the art of governing; Machiavelli's *The Prince* was an early model. In Spain, Juan de Castillo y Aguayo's *El perfecto rigidor (The Perfect Magistrate)* had appeared in 1586, Gracian Dantisco's *Galateo español* in 1593, and even the aphorisms of Socrates on governing had been translated into Spanish (RIQ, 155). Men's affairs were now clearly in the hands of men, not of a divine arbiter. How such rulers should behave became an issue of paramount importance. Don Quixote's advice, which begins in this chapter, is among the best written on the subject. Not only does it apply to men in office, but to all men required to direct the actions of others. [Cervantes' concepts are sometimes far ahead of those held even in our own times. For

example, "Never to be guided by arbitrary law" (739) is a maxim
still consistently ignored by authority from the teacher to the
policeman.] Whereas Sancho excels in practical matters, Don
Quixote's advice is a model of excellence in the abstract. The
knight's words remind us at times of Polonius (for Don Quixote
is himself something of a windbag) and at times of Portia in her
speech on mercy. Shakespeare and Cervantes were heirs of the
same tradition. Furthermore, Cervantes, like his hero, had had
experience with the authorities and could have wished them to
have had more pity, more understanding, and more impartiality.
Don Quixote's advice is, in effect, a powerful plea for good government given by a man who cannot govern himself to a man
about to govern nothing at all. Yet it exceeds in wisdom the
practice of the large majority of actual rulers in the world. Cervantes once again shows us that this man, mad though he may
be, is no more so than those who call themselves sane—like governors who take bribes or who are guided by selfish motives.

Chapter 43

Cervantes tells us that Don Quixote's "acts discredited his
judgment and his judgment his acts." (740) It is the instinct of
genius, however, not to belabor this point in exposition. Rather
Cervantes shows us how such a personality operates in his relations in the everyday world.

Whereas the previous chapter has stressed precepts, this one
stresses behavior. But teaching Sancho how to behave is a thankless job, and even Don Quixote seems to be sometimes amused
at the whole procedure. He spouts proverbs just as steadfastly as
Don Quixote tries to suppress them. Teaching Sancho to use
eruct instead of *belch* is like trying to teach Dapple the alphabet.
Although he has warned Sancho against affectation, Don Quixote's
lessons on etiquette seem sometimes to be aimed at disguising
the peasant in him. But as Sancho points out, his only fortune is

proverbs, and if he is to be a good governor, he must be himself and not someone in disguise. Despite Don Quixote's excellent grasp of abstract matters, Sancho, in all his innocence, is better equipped to govern himself than his master is to govern him. For example, his illiteracy, as Sancho shrewdly sees, will not be alleviated by his learning to sign his name. Better to dismiss the whole business of writing by feigning a paralyzed hand.

Chapter 44

This chapter marks the beginning of Sancho's governorship and the concurrent development of two separate plots. Cervantes now shifts back and forth from Sancho on his isle to Don Quixote at the Duke's castle. He seems more conscious of technique in the 1615 *Quixote* than in the earlier book. For example, Cide Hamete explains the reason for the omission of digressions in this book—so that the episodes may all arise from the actual events themselves (746). Sancho's governorship is such an episode, and continuity is maintained by shifting back to the Duke's castle at intervals. This counterpoint technique, polished and refined, is, of course, common in the twentieth-century novel. Furthermore, it is possible to discern interesting parallels between events on Sancho's isle and the occurrences at the castle; these parallels add to the unifying effect of the counterpoint technique. For instance, Sancho's ruling passion, to govern, is mocked by the "great escort" which accompanies him to his isle at the same time as Don Quixote's ruling passion, Dulcinea, is mocked by the courting of Altisidora. Don Quixote slams the window at the end of this chapter in much the same spirit in which Sancho fires the doctor near the outset of his rule. And Don Quixote's view of himself as "a gentleman of birth" beset by the indignity of poverty fits neatly with Sancho's assertion of identity on arriving on his isle, "I'm no Don, and there has never been a Don in my whole family" (755). These parallels contrast with the book's central dichotomy, that between mind and matter, spirit and body, which is implicit in the two main characters.

At the end of the chapter Don Quixote is thrown into a fright by the advances of Altisidora, a fright not allayed by the Duchess's assurances that the Don's modesty would be respected by herself and her staff. Sancho, however, at the beginning of his ordeal, exudes self-assurance by promising that within four days he will "weed out these Dons" who are, in his words, "as tiresome as gnats." (755)

Chapter 45

A mock heroic invocation to the sun, suggesting that a new canto has started, is a fitting opening for the episode of Sancho's governorship. It is a canto which introduces Sancho as master, mocking and reversing the order which has already been established in the knight-squire relationship. As we have seen, the entire question of governing and governorship was of particular significance for Renaissance man. But although Sancho wears the dress of a lawyer, he replaces the windy generalizations and jargon of the treatises on governing with good common sense and action; he astonishes everyone with his "judicious decisions" (760). All three of the cases Sancho tries in this chapter involve disputes over money; only one of them involves a plaintiff who is himself innocent and only one involves sex. Thus Cervantes represents the courts of the world. Sancho's judgments are fair and perceptive. He possesses an instinctive understanding of people and of their behavior, a mother wit. In the light of his successful resolutions of the cases, we forget the mockery underlying the entire situation, the mockery symbolized in the invocation at the opening of the chapter. Again Sancho has turned the tables on the Duke and the Duchess; for his own justice is far superior to the kind of justice dispensed by those who use the demented and the innocent for their diversions. It is they who now appear the real subjects for mockery.

And yet Sancho's office is ironically dependent on those who are his moral inferiors. Barely more than a puppet manipulated by puppeteers, he is a symbol of man, situated in an uncomprehensible universe and controlled by alien gods. Within these limits, he establishes a temporary hall of real justice; but like Don Quixote, he is unable to create anything permanent. Don Quixote is caught in the cobwebs of his own brain and Sancho in the miasma of his credulity, so that the virtue represented by each is fruitless. All the wisdom of a Minos is squandered in a world of practical jokes.

Still, the ambiguities of Cervantes' genius lead us on, for Sancho himself would be the first to appreciate a good practical joke, and he himself would disown the title of Minos as quickly as he had rejected "Don Sancho Panza." However, the manipulation by the Duke and Duchess is unpleasant because Sancho and Don Quixote do not *know*, are not "in on the joke." Pathetically they seem to *sense* that they are a source of laughter for their hosts. They are indeed representative of man confronting the absurd, which they are unable to overcome, to recognize, or to handle.

Chapter 46

From Sancho's isle, we move back to the castle and to Don Quixote's encounter with "certain cats and bells" (760). Sancho is mentioned only once in the chapter, when the Duchess sends a page to Teresa with his letters and a bundle of clothes, thus creating a new diversion for the court. Sancho's governing is as staunch as Don Quixote's loyalty to Dulcinea. Although both are merely pawns in a kind of court masque put on by "the noble pair," both succeed within the limits imposed by the directors of the masque. They succeed on two levels: 1) each upholds his own ideals—Sancho, common sense, and Don Quixote, fidelity to the chivalric code; 2) each succeeds in the role in which he is cast by the directors, thereby providing amusement for the audience. True, the episode with the cats misfires when Don Quixote is forced to take to his bed for five days, but this is the fault of the directors. For once the Duke and Duchess seem genuinely concerned, for it would never do to lose the leading actor; the curtain must temporarily be drawn.

All of this underlines the question of role and of identity, the problem of "the play," which vitally interested Renaissance man. Although Don Quixote and Sancho have succeeded as actors in the Duke's masque and in their own "play," a chivalric romance about a knight and his squire, they have failed miserably to recognize themselves and their own actual roles for what they are. Cervantes emphasizes this point with the play motif. It is fitting that the Knight of the Mirrors should be Don Quixote's antagonist in the 1615 *Quixote,* for his mirrors symbolically offer Don Quixote a means of seeing himself as he is. The scratching by the cat is only another in the string of disasters which are a result of Don Quixote's confusion of reality and role. Although the world *may* be a stage, no man can play three roles simultaneously without creating chaos; he is Quixada; he thinks he is Quixote; the Duke and Duchess think he is a madman. An integrated person knows who he is and appears to others as he is, at least to a large degree. As the 1615 *Quixote* progresses we see the degradation to which Don Quixote's confusion of role leads him, a degradation symbolized here by his becoming the innocent and unwitting victim of the cat, which is, in effect, about as civilized as "the noble pair" themselves.

Chapter 47

While Don Quixote is being tempted by the artful Altisidora, Sancho is being tempted by his own *femme fatale,* food.
Between him and his meal, however, stands a doctor, presumably devoted to his governor's welfare. Sancho is put in the position of Tantalus, from whom food was snatched just before the
moment of his tasting it. Delightful dishes are set before the
Governor only to be removed; finally a letter arrives from the
Duke warning of the danger of poisoning and ordering Sancho to
"eat nothing that is set before you" (768). At this point the table
is cleared. Frustration mounts as a peasant appears to ask Sancho
for 600 ducats as "dowry" for his son who would marry the
daughter of a very rich farmer, a daughter who is missing ten
teeth and whose knees meet her mouth. Hungry and penniless,
Sancho explodes into anger, threatening to break the peasant's
head open with a chair.

It is this series of events which marks the beginning of
Sancho's disillusionment with governing an isle. Twice he hints
that he is about to give up: first, when he says that a job that will
not feed a man "isn't worth two beans" (767), and later, when
he has an inkling that his governorship will not last (769).

Sancho's vulnerable point, his stomach, is well-known; to
attack him there is to court rebellion. Whereas Don Quixote has
been assaulted inwardly by Altisidora, Sancho is assaulted physically by being deprived of food. To divert Don Quixote from
thoughts of Dulcinea (as Altisidora threatens) is the equivalent
of starving Sancho. This chapter and the preceding one go hand
in hand, yet Altisidora is never a serious rival of Dulcinea or a
real temptation. And because of the inward nature of Don
Quixote's problem, he can meet it with "a deep sigh," whereas
for Sancho the wait until supper is interminable. It is perhaps
this frustration which marks the beginning of Sancho's acknowl-
edgement of his identity as a peasant, or at least of his identity as

a squire. We can say he is starved into sanity. Don Quixote's cure is not so simple, however, and the counterpoint continues.

Chapter 48

As the 1615 story progresses, nothing becomes more apparent than Don Quixote's growing fears. Much of the confidence and brave spirit of the earlier episodes seem to have ebbed away, leaving Don Quixote prey to his enchanters, who become increasingly malign. In this chapter, Don Quixote's terror at the appearance of the waiting woman, Doña Rodriguez, and his fears of those who pinch him contrast sharply with the self-confident attitude he displayed, for example, in the bedroom scene at his home in Chapter 1 of this book. Rather than aggressiveness, he now displays a passive bewilderment as he shrinks deeper into his bed. The bed, in fact, is a suitable retreat from his growing confusions, and Don Quixote remains there throughout Doña Rodriguez's entire recital of her woes. His withdrawal into the bed represents a desire to escape; he seems to feel safe only beneath its covers. Nor does he hurry to assure the waiting woman of his assistance in her plight as he had assured, for example, the Princess Micomicona. Instead he is easily sidetracked into a discussion of the Duchess's sores. Don Quixote's knightly attitude has clearly suffered from this chain of disasters. It is now apparent only in his talk, when he assures the waiting woman that the Duchess's sores must distill "liquid ambergris." (779) Although we have admired him for his brave attempts to act according to his ideals, now in his perplexity he seems merely pitiful. This perplexity however, will eventually lead to a recognition of his true identity, a recognition which tragically comes too late. Both Sancho on his isle and Don Quixote in his bed have been thrown into violent confusion. Sancho's confusion is more easily resolved since it depends largely on the satisfaction of his bodily needs. Even his anger with the peasant is related more to his empty stomach and consequent feeling of frustration than to his sense of justice or injustice.

More telling, however, is the tragi-comic scene in Don Quixote's bedroom in which the waiting woman sits "without taking off her spectacles or putting down her candle" (775), recounting her troubled life to a knight clothed in bedding so that only his face shows (thereby parodying the knight clothed in armor). He has exchanged his helmet and breastplate for a quilt. Furthermore, Doña Rodriguez herself is, as Riquer shows, an ignorant and crack-brained woman, who, like the Priest, has been excluded from the joke on Don Quixote and who in her foolishness believes that Don Quixote is a knight who will defend her daughter's honor (RIQ, 151). She is another foil for him.

To order an attack on this bedroom (because the Duchess's vanity has been wounded) is like setting dogs on a sick animal. The Duke and Duchess's tricks show that they stand for the very opposite of the ideals that Don Quixote once undertook to defend. The terror lies in the fact that, whereas Don Quixote has been unsuccessful, "the noble pair" are able to put their immoralities into action; it is perhaps this terror that Don Quixote senses—the wanton and destructive whims of a self-indulgent "nobility." His own nobility is morally a far greater one, though totally ineffectual. Like the lady in Doña Rodriguez' tale, one feels the Duchess would indeed be capable of running a bodkin into Don Quixote's back.

Chapter 49

Sancho's initial doubts of his ability to assume a governorship having been dispelled by an evening meal of beef hash and onions, he is ready to make his nightly rounds of the isle. Let them look to my feeding, Sancho says, "which is the main point of the matter, and the most important" (781). Don Quixote's situation is far more complex and not to be simplified by a plate

of beef hash and onions. His needs can be satisfied only in some
other world. The fast is a stimulus to Don Quixote as food is to
Sancho; only after his meal does Sancho proclaim a set of principles for his governorship: to favor laboring men, protect gentlemen's privileges, reward the virtuous, respect religion, and honor
the clergy. Whereas Don Quixote's code—to defend maidens,
relieve widows, succor orphans and the needy (87)—cuts across
all strata of society, Sancho's code is one which recognizes the
existing social structure. As a practical politician, Sancho recognizes the laboring class, the gentleman, and the clergy, promising
to protect the rights of all in different ways. However, like the
pronouncements of most politicians, his code perhaps contains
a contradiction, for in protecting gentlemen's privileges he may
do a disfavor to the laboring man.

*   *   *

Of the three cases Sancho encounters this evening only two
have been contrived by the Duke and the Duchess; the third one
takes everyone by surprise. The first is another quarrel over
money between two men who have just left a gambling house.
Sancho swears he will eliminate all gambling houses although his
clerk points out that since gambling is not likely to be erased,
Sancho would do better to direct his efforts against the houses of
poor quality where men are outrageously cheated. The second is
a rather aimless episode (as most of the Duke's pranks are) concerning a youth with a clever tongue. The point of the encounter
seems to be the repartee rather than a crime, and Sancho, tiring
of this mockery of the law, dismisses the youth with a warning.

The episode which is not contrived concerns a young girl,
who, weary of her virtual imprisonment by her severe father,
cajoles her brother into lending her his clothes for a night so
that she may see life in the village. The brother meanwhile is
found abroad in his sister's clothes. Both are overcome with embarrassment, and Sancho and his staff return them to their home.
That fact is stranger than fiction is clear from these cases. The
Duke's and Duchess's imaginary situations, like their lives, have
centered on money and its consequences, but the real case in-

volves a problem of individual freedom, freedom denied the girl
by her father. Even more interesting is the mystery of the brother,
whose reason for wearing his sister's clothes is not explaind.

Sancho is thrown into the role of Don Quixote, of assisting
maidens in distress, but his assistance is of a different variety from
that of his master. He tells the girl that she has been involved in
a childish prank and that there is no need for all this sighing and
sobbing. One can imagine Don Quixote springing to the saddle
of Rocinante to avenge a weeping lady. But Sancho is a father
himself and perhaps sees in the girl his own Sanchica. It is the
ability of Sancho to relate to everyday life that makes him a good
governor, and Don Quixote's inability to see the world as it is
that prevents him from being an effective knight.

Chapter 50

In Chapter 50 we return to Don Quixote, who gives his explanation of the pinching episode; he maintains that a group of
phantoms was responsible, whereas it was actually the work of
Altisidora and the Duchess herself, who is not above petty revenge on her waiting woman and the innocent knight. The
Duchess's hidden ulcers are symbolic of her underlying ugly and
festering disposition. And the Duke is "greatly amused" when he
learns Don Quixote has once more been fooled and beaten.

* * *

Teresa and Sanchica are also fooled in this chapter by the
Duchess who sends her page to them with a letter and beads. Not
content with the prey at hand, the Duke and Duchess extend their
joke to Sancho's family. Teresa has no doubts of her husband's
governorship and at once adopts the role of governor's lady to
the best of her ability. Her first thought concerns clothes, "a
hooped farthingale"; her second, a trip to court in a coach.

Teresa's innocent credulity is underlined by the skepticism expressed by Sampson Carrasco and the priest when they are told.
Whereas her native wit informs her that Sampson is "a bit of a
joker," and she refuses to let him write answers to her letters, she
never for a moment doubts the word of the Duchess. The suit of
clothes and the beads brought by the page are convincing enough
for her. One of the most unattractive aspects of the pranks of the
Duke and Duchess is that they use their noble station, which
should carry with it a sense of serious responsibility and concern
for others, to deceive Don Quixote, Sancho, and Teresa into accepting their jokes at face value. Instead of following the precept
of "noblesse oblige," the Duke and Duchess practice deception
based on an inner sense of their own superiority and their right
to exploit others for their own pleasure.

Chapter 51

We return once more to Sancho on his isle, subsisting on a
diet of dried fruit and four gulps of cold water. Sancho's men-
tality is not so limited that he cannot curse both the governorship
and its donor for thwarting his appetite. But despite his hunger,
when a case sounding like a riddle comes before him, he parries
it with good common sense. Furthermore, the ordinances which
he lays down are ones modern governors might study with profit,
especially his appointment of an inspector of the poor to discover
whether or not they are feigning poverty.

Of course, Sancho's isle is no "isle" at all, merely a town
named Barataria, but this discrepancy seems to bother neither
Sancho nor the perpetrators of the hoax, for the terms of Quixote's
chivalric fantasy are such that the nature of things may be
changed at will. The characters as well as the reader are all too
ready to "suspend disbelief"; Don Quixote's dream is contagious
to all who come into contact with it. Furthermore, Sancho is ignorant of the meaning of *insula,* an archaic word for *island* fre-

quently employed in *Amadis of Gaul* and other books of chivalry, which is the reason Don Quixote uses it (RIQ, 155). Thus he is easily convinced that the little town in Aragon is the "island" of Barataria, a name which comes from the Spanish *barato* meaning cheap, for Sancho's governorship is one which, as he learns, has been too cheaply won.

* * *

The exchange of letters in these chapters foreshadows the epistolary technique of later novels and supplies the first communication between master and squire since Sancho took office. Don Quixote's letter to Sancho contains several surprising remarks. Until now he has thought all enchanters to be hostile. Now for the first time he writes that some of his enchanters defend him. This is one of the early harbingers of his eventual return to sanity. Furthermore, we learn that Don Quixote intends soon "to leave this idle life" (801). "I must comply," he writes, "with my profession rather than with their pleasures" (802). Plato is a friend, but truth is a better friend, he tells Sancho in Latin. Here is clear proof that Don Quixote is now at least partially aware of his real role as an entertainer in this household. Had he seen himself as a noble guest, he would not have felt it necessary to call this life "idle," for the Duke and Duchess have supplied him with numerous opportunities to exercise his knight-errantry. But it is clear from his letter that now Don Quixote, like Sancho, is playing the game of "the noble pair" on a temporary basis. (Since Sancho is Don Quixote's only real confidant, the letter is essential, now that Sancho is away, in order to reveal Don Quixote's inner motivations. Letters provide the novel with new angles by which a character may be viewed.)

Why Don Quixote should wish to play the game at all is another question. This brief respite from the hardships of the road has been all too tempting to resist. Shelter, food, and comforts are provided in return for his acting the buffoon. Abandoning for the moment his high-minded quest, he has undertaken to become a clown or a court jester. For Sancho the role is more natural, but for him too it is an embarrassment to be the butt of someone else's jokes. The fault, then, does not lie entirely with the Duke and the Duchess, for they have obtained the tacit consent of their victims in return for material advantages. The entire stay at the castle is a travesty of Don Quixote's original intentions. It marks another step toward the degeneration of his mission and the rejection of his identity as "knight."

Chapter 52

Don Quixote at last announces his intention to leave the castle, for he now finds everything there "clean contrary to the rule of knighthood" (804), but one final challenge is presented to him. Doña Rodriguez, stating more truthfully than she knows, that it is impossible "to expect justice from the Duke" (805), begs Don Quixote's help for her daughter, who has been wronged by her lover. Once more Don Quixote takes up the gauntlet; it is as if one more lesson, added to the earlier ones, might effect his cure. And the Duke undertakes to provide a worthy opponent, one of his lackeys. (One of the hard and fast rules of knight-errantry which Don Quixote was fond of quoting to Sancho in the 1605 *Quixote* was that knights never took arms against those inferior to them in station. The Duke is incapable of recognizing this principle himself, for he is always ready to take advantage of the Don's inferior status.)

In the meantime two letters arrive from Teresa Panza, one containing the all too appropriate malapropism, "your Pomposity," in referring to the Duchess; the other addressed to Sancho but opened by Don Quixote and read to the assembled company. The ducal pair will stop at nothing, even at reading private mail, to insure their entertainment. Teresa's letter gives clear proof of the cruelty of the tricks played upon Sancho and her. Her dreams of going to court, her staunch faith in the goodness of the Duchess, the provincial gossip she relates, make one wish the Duchess had chosen someone of her own status to ridicule. The pain of disappointment which Teresa is about to experience will be the result of a wanton prank which she could not understand if she tried. And since Teresa is not implicated like her husband in matters of knight-errantry, her injury as a bystander is all the more cruel. This chapter and the next describe the ultimate lengths to which the Duke and Duchess will go to produce situations that are comic to them but tragic to the omniscient author and reader.

Chapter 53

The chapter opens with one of Cervantes' rare homilies—this one on the nature of time. Everything, he tells us, evolves in cycles, and change is the only constant value in life. Human life speeds on "without hope of renewal" (811).

Sancho's governorship is also subject to change. The way in which it is brought to an end, however, is the indirect result of a practical joke to reduce Sancho to the form and level of a tortoise. It has already been noted in the 1615 *Quixote* that Cervantes continually uses animals as counterparts of men. Thus Sancho, encased in two huge shields and unable to bend his knees, falls down and is forced to draw his head in as protection from those who trample and stumble over him in the mock battle for his isle. He virtually becomes a tortoise.

Once freed he faints away, but he has learned his lesson. He is grieved to think of his previous ambition and pride and goes at once to saddle Dapple for the journey back to the Duke's castle. It is clear now that Sancho is well aware of the nature of his governorship, for he swears, "These tricks aren't to be played twice" (815). Although he still apparently reveres "the Duke, my lord" (815), as he calls him, the people on the isle, particularly the doctor who has starved him, now appear no better than scoundrels, and he cannot wait to leave them and to return to "steady walking."

The tramplings in the later pages of *Don Quixote* become more and more numerous and more and more painful both to the persons receiving them and to the reader. (A tortoise is a reptile found in muddy and low-lying places. Its name comes from the Latin *tortus* (twisted), a reference to the feet.) Having been reduced to a reptilian state by those on his isle, Sancho can still reply to his steward, paraphrasing the words of Job, "Naked came I out of my mother's womb, and naked shall I return thither." (1:21) Like Job, Sancho has suffered without understanding the reasons for it, for, as he says, "I governed like an angel." (815). The Duke's and Duchess's wanton exercise of their sense of humor resembles the whims of an incomprehensible deity. But to compare Job and Sancho at all is to move from the sublime to the ridiculous. Job made his statement after learning of the death of his sons; Sancho uttered his after he had learned who he was, after the death of the 'Lord Governor' within him. He will undergo pain and humiliation no longer, but will return, ironically, to the Duke—the originator of the various disasters that have befallen him on his isle. At the same time, as Riquer notes, in all the episodes concerning Sancho's governorship, Cervantes has been satirizing ambition (RIQ, 156). Thus the key theme, that of self-knowledge, is often accompanied by Cervantes' ironic social commentary.

Chapter 54

Cervantes returns us, for one paragraph, to the castle, where we learn that preparations for combat between Quixote and the Gascon lackey proceed apace. This paragraph serves to remind the reader that the castle is still the focal point in the plot although we are temporarily removed from it.

The purpose of Sancho's meeting with Ricote, the Moor, is twofold. First, it shows that Sancho has learned his lesson well; the lure of gold no longer holds as much power over him. He refuses Ricote's offer of two hundred crowns in return for his help, saying, "I'm not at all greedy" (821). He even talks of principles—of not committing treason by favoring the king's enemies, the Moors. Second, it shows that Sancho has achieved some measure of self-awareness. The company of Don Quixote, Cervantes tells us, "gave him more pleasure than the governorship of all the isles in the world" (816), and Sancho says to Ricote that he is "no good at governing." (821) His love for Don Quixote is the main reason for his refusal to accompany Ricote. Without the Ricote episode we would have nothing by which to measure the extent of Sancho's new insights.

Cervantes also uses this episode to comment on Moors in seventeenth-century Spain. Ousted from their homes by proclamations of Philip III in 1609 and 1613, the Moors had been forced to flee to other countries—France, Italy, Germany, and Barbary, for example. Like Ricote's, many families had been separated, and Ricote himself must travel in disguise as a pilgrim; nevertheless, he loves and weeps for Spain. Strangely enough, Ricote seems to feel that the proclamation was a wise and just one, for he says that many of his people are indeed desperate and foolish, that exile is a mild and merciful penalty. As we saw in the 1605 *Quixote* in the episode of the captive and Zoraida, Cervantes himself shares the national feeling against Moors. Sancho's refusal to help Ricote dig his treasure is adamant, and although he promises not to betray Ricote, it is clear that he wants little to do with this "enemy of Spain," although he has shared food and drink with him and calls him "my friend" (822). It is also highly unlikely that in real life a Ricote would have upheld the King's proclamation against his people and himself with such fervor. But because he defames his fellow Moors, Ricote is depicted as basically a "good fellow." In the same way, Zoraida became acceptable only after she had denied her own people by adopting Christianity and changing her name. We feel the national animus influencing Cervantes' portrayal of Ricote, Sancho, and Zoraida.

Chapter 55

Sancho's own descent into the underworld occurs in this chapter. Having nearly arrived at the Duke's castle, both he and Dapple fall into a deep pit. Sancho is reminded of "the cave of that enchanted Montesinos" (823), but instead of by the objects of Don Quixote's bright fantasies, he is entertained by snakes and toads. It is a place which inspires Sancho with the utmost terror. However, symbolically it serves the same function as Don Quixote's descent, for it suggests the spiraling downward motion of this book, a book in which Don Quixote and Sancho are downgraded, trampled, and "buried alive," but eventually are resurrected.

A certain student residing at the court of the Duke sees Sancho's fall as a punishment meted out for bad government. But Sancho is not about to assume guilt for sins he has not committed. Like the scholar at the cave of Montesinos, this student is no match for Sancho, who tells him, "God understands me, and that's enough" (827).

The main difference between the two visits to the underworld is that Don Quixote's is voluntary, like the trips to the underworld of epic heroes, and Sancho's is not. Don Quixote is carefully lowered onto his ledge, whereas Sancho tumbles onto his. One is in the nature of an adventure, the other of a mishap. Sancho's is more painful, and upon emerging, he can state with new insight that he does not give a farthing about being a governor. In a sense the student is right. Although Sancho is not being punished for being a bad governor, the fall symbolizes that fall all undergo who think that they are someone they are not. Through his suffering as a tortoise and in the pit, Sancho has learned his rightful identity, whereas Don Quixote has emerged from his cave even more deeply entangled in his fantasies of knighthood.

Chapter 56

Like so many of the battles in *Don Quixote,* the one in defense of Doña Rodriguez' daughter misfires. It is placed at the end
of the hero's stay with the Duke as a kind of climax to the entire
visit. Cupid, who shoots Tosilos with one of his arrows, renders
the lackey helpless before Don Quixote can complete his charge.
He and Rocinante are arrested in mid-career. It is an appropriate
conclusion to the visit with the Duke and Duchess which has, in
effect, also arrested Don Quixote in mid-career. We have seen
him for the past twenty-six chapters in a series of still shots: listen-
ing to the Countess Trifaldi; sitting astride Clavileño, who remains stationary; lying in bed while Doña Rodriguez recites her
woes. His role has been a passive one. Now when he attempts to
charge Tosilos in the lists of the Duke, he is faced with an opponent who will not meet his attack. This is a culminating frustration in the whole series of tricks which have been played on him.
Even the spectators are "depressed and sad," although the princi-
pals in the affair, Tosilos and Doña Rodriguez' daughter, are well
enough satisfied. That the business temporarily turns out well is
no direct consequence of Don Quixote's actions, only a by-product.
No matter how hard Don Quixote tries, his efforts are somehow
muted and diverted from their original intention. The whole
visit with the Duke and Duchess has consisted of purposeless
action, much like the scene at the inn in the 1605 *Quixote* in
which the Don is caught for a night standing on Rocinante with
his wrist tied to the bolt of a hay-loft door. But unlike Maritornes in that episode, the Duke and Duchess have not been satisfied to play only one trick of this sort. Once again Quixote is
forced to make peace with himself by blaming "wicked enchanters" with the transformation of his opponent. That he has
been thwarted this time by Cupid himself is perhaps a commentary on his own idealism concerning love, for he has persistently
thwarted Cupid, allowing neither Altisidora nor any other maiden

to move him. The union of the lovers in this chapter is the work of Cupid and chance, not of Don Quixote, and we see that like ourselves, Don Quixote, is condemned to "ever drifting in uncertainty, driven from end to end." (Pascal, *Pensées*, New York, 1941, p. 25.) Don Quixote's frustration is threefold: 1) he has been denied battle; 2) the opponent he expected does not even appear; 3) he is forced by deception to bear arms against a lackey, a man of inferior status.

Chapter 57

Despite the silly practical jokes which have filled the preceding pages, it should be said that the Duke has at least been generous in providing for the physical needs of his guests. As Don Quixote and Sancho prepare to leave, Sancho is given two hundred gold crowns and saddle bags full of provisions. And some of the worst tricks, like the farewell song of Altisidora, have originated with the servants, not with the Duke or Duchess. The Duchess professes to be astonished at the effrontery of Altisidora's song.

It should also be noted, however, that the money was given to Sancho and not to Don Quixote. Sancho has just finished repeating his line from *Job*, "Naked I was born, naked I am now" (834), and congratulating himself on a clean conscience when we learn of his stuffed purse and saddle bags. Sancho never fails to take advantage of a windfall; to have offered Don Quixote two hundred crowns would have been an insult which the Duke is at least sensitive enough to perceive. Although these pages have shown the ducal pair in a dark light, they do have redeeming features and certain ethical standards by which they attempt to live. Their flaw, significantly enough, seems to be their passion for the game of knight-errantry on a more literal level than it is played by Don Quixote. The Don parries the Duke's parting challenge over the matter of Altisidora's garters, refusing to fight his eager patron and thus depriving the Duke of one final exploit. For Don Quixote knight-errantry is not a "game," and herein lies the vast difference between him and the Duke. Cervantes seems to say that life is a more serious affair than petty Dukes and Duchesses are capable of imagining. It is Don Quixote who shows the good sense and good judgment in this parting scene.

Chapter 58

Once free of the Duke and Duchess, Don Quixote and Sancho find themselves again on the road. Don Quixote preaches on the value of liberty; obligations, he tells his squire, are "bonds that curb a free spirit" (837). However, on learning of the two hundred gold crowns, Don Quixote abandons his sermon. Like his squire, he is glad to have the money despite his principles.

The chapter consists of two encounters, the first with the bearers of four statues of saints. The central theme of the 1615 *Quixote* has been the question of identity. Statues, like mirrors and plays, reflect images. The message of these statues is quite clear to Don Quixote. They knew who they were and what they were fighting for—St. George, St. Martin, St. James, St. Paul— "but up till now I do not know what I am conquering" (839) says Don Quixote in discouragement. At least he is becoming aware of the lack of direction in his mission and is, therefore, more ready to deal with it. His present attitude is a far cry indeed from his certainty in the 1605 *Quixote:* "I know who I am and I know, too, that I am capable of being . . . all the Twelve Peers of France. . . ." (54) Don Quixote's doubts continue to mount as the 1615 *Quixote* draws to an end.

The second encounter in the chapter does nothing to reassure him. A pastoral scene unfolds, an outing of rich young people, who take pleasure in netting small birds (the same sort of cruel and whimsical activity often indulged in at the Duke's castle.) In an attempt to repay the group for his meal, Don

Quixote undertakes to defend the beauty of two shepherdesses among them. He suffers his first trampling as a result. The challenge he offers is a superfluous one; no reason exists to uphold the beauty of the two maidens. But Don Quixote will not be put off and plants himself in the middle of the highway. The play of the shepherds and shepherdesses is equally without issue but somewhat less dangerous to life and limb. Don Quixote, Sancho, and their mounts are borne down under the feet of a herd of bulls. This is another instance of failure and humiliation, a defeat devoid of purpose or reason brought about by a herd of animals. The 1615 *Quixote* is marked by a series of such descents foreshadowing Don Quixote's final unhorsing and descent into his grave. As a victim of the Duke and Duchess, Don Quixote was at least dealing with characters who could partially share his fantasy; as a victim of bulls, Don Quixote, the knight, is an irrelevant detail.

The pastoral scene also foreshadows a turn which Don Quixote's own life is to move toward temporarily. But as we see in the rather foolish amusement of these young people, the pastoral life is artificial and frivolous, no substitute for the knight-errantry which Don Quixote envisages but is never able to realize.

Chapter 59

The discouragement of Don Quixote is such that he refuses to eat at the next meal, his reaction to frustration being exactly opposite that of Sancho, who crams himself full of bread and cheese. Nothing illustrates better the fact that each man's nature basically has not changed. Master and squire have in no sense switched parts; their behavior has only been modified in certain ways by experience and by their association. Thus Sancho has gained in wisdom and Don Quixote in self-knowledge. But to see knight and squire as each taking on the role of the other

is to misstate and oversimplify the very complex and subtle
changes in their characters which occur as the novel progresses.
Sancho remains oriented toward the physical world, Don Quixote
toward the metaphysical, even though he concludes, after being
persuaded by Sancho to take a bite of food, that his squire reasons "more like a philosopher than a fool" (848). Still, Sancho is
extremely hesitant about lashing himself, not seeing, as Don
Quixote professes to, that any principle is involved.

At the end of the chapter Cervantes cleverly jeers at the imposter who has attempted to write a sequel to the 1605 *Quixote*.
The problem involved here is that of authentic versus inauthen-
tic history. Cervantes claims that his book, which he calls a *history*, is the authentic one, and yet both his *Don Quixote* and
Avellaneda's are books of *fiction*, so neither one can really tell
the "truth." Thus, Cervantes' continual references to this
spurious second book are made partly to convince the reader that
Don Quixote actually lived and that his "true" life differs from
the "false" one invented by the imposter. He is also satirizing
historians who deliberately falsified their work, a common practice in the sixteenth and seventeenth centuries. For example,
Cervantes reminds us that Avellaneda had Don Quixote renounce
Dulcinea and adopt the title, "el caballero desamorado" (the un-
loving knight), a fact that fills Don Quixote with "furious
indignation." (OB, 1031)

Bruce Wardropper has shown that the very definition of the
novel suggests an ambiguity in the relation between the real and
the imaginary. *Don Quixote,* as the first example of the novel
genre, demonstrates this ambiguity in many ways, especially
through the hero, whose madness lies in the fact that he cannot
distinguish between imaginary events in books he has read and
real events that have happened. Wardropper claims that Cervantes
cultivates this same madness in the reader, thus re-creating the
human dilemma which, through mimesis, he has transformed into
the madness of Don Quixote. (WARD, 1-11) For truth may be
discovered at the very heart of illusion and vice-versa.

Cervantes has already dealt with the imposter history of
Avellaneda in the Prologue to the 1615 *Quixote*. Clearly it is a
fraud, for Don Quixote glances at it and sees that some words in

the prologue are questionable, the language is Aragonese, and Sancho's wife is called Mari Gutierrez. This last point is of some interest since Cervantes himself has changed Teresa's name from Juana Gutierrez in the 1605 *Quixote.* (See SP, 47) Cervantes is never above parodying himself, but Don Quixote's reasons for judging the imposter an ignoramus are rather petty ones; Cervantes is satirizing critics who judge a book on some minor point like a change in name. He kills two birds with one stone: 1) he shows the imposter to be inaccurate having Don Quixote even change his itinerary from Saragossa to Barcelona to make him twice inaccurate; and 2) he mocks his own critics who doubtless will not be reticent about mentioning such discrepancies as the change in Teresa's name.

Furthermore, Sancho's vanity has been wounded by the imposter, who has portrayed him as a guzzler and a fool. Sancho looks into the mirror that fiction holds up to him and seeing a half-truth, is more hurt than he would be by a falsehood. Once again we are faced with the question of what is authentic, what is truth. As Coleridge said in a pronouncement worthy of Sancho, "No simile runs on all four legs." Thus Avellaneda's Sancho is a guzzler and a fool, whereas Sancho sees himself as a simple and droll fellow. In this way Cervantes suggests the many-faceted nature of truth. The very fact that Sancho sees himself as "droll" proves that he is not such a "fool" as Avellaneda may believe him to be, for it indicates that his humor is often conscious and not the result of stupid blunders. On the other hand, if this were the entire truth, Sancho would lose part of the simplicity to which he lays claim. In this manner Cervantes shows us that any point of view affords only partial insights, even a man's judgment of his own qualities. And surely Avellaneda is closer to the truth than Sancho when it comes to the matter of "guzzling." The humor in the passage springs from Sancho's vehemence in denying an assertion about himself which is clearly accurate in part. To what subtle ends Cervantes uses the imposter's history is evident.

Chapter 60

The only instance of Sancho's fighting and overcoming Don
Quixote is related in this chapter; it illustrates the new-found
sense of role that Sancho has discovered as the result of his governorship and its failure. " 'I depose no King, I make no King,' "
says Sancho, " 'but help myself who am my own lord.' " (856)
Sancho has remained an attendant and underling long enough;
he has now come to realize that he is his own best salvation. But
he asserts his identity only in self-defense against Don Quixote's
attempt to lash him for Dulcinea's disenchantment. He does not
do it to set himself up as lord and master in Don Quixote's place;
in fact, a few minutes later he is calling Don Quixote for help as
he feels the feet of the "dead" bandits hanging in the trees.
Sancho is a symbol of the common man of the Renaissance who
is discovering himself and his rights and has begun to assert himself but still continues to look to the nobility for protection.
Sancho's overcoming of Don Quixote may be seen as a harbinger
of the social revolution which occurred during the centuries following the Renaissance, a revolution bringing rule and control
by an effete nobility, founded on divine right and birth, to an end.

*   *   *

Roque Guinart, who is introduced in this chapter, is based
on an actual contemporary figure, Perot Rocaguinarda, who was
33 at the time of the publication of the second part of *Quixote*.
(OB, 1036) Roque Guinart is an adventurer, who must be distinguished from the *picaro* as he appears in the seventeenth-
century picaresque tale. Alexander A. Parker, in *Literature and
the Delinquent,* states that *picaro* was a word describing "an of-
fender against moral and civil laws" (not a gangster or a mur-
derer) (PL, 4). The *picaro,* of whom we have an example in Gines
de Pasamonte (Master Peter), usually came from a disreputable

milieu of cheaters and thieves. He was "low, vicious, deceitful, dishonourable and shameless" (PL, 4).

But Roque Guinart is not this sort of character. Don Quixote addresses him as "Sir Roque." Like Robin Hood, he redistributes money gathered from his victims, rights wrongs done to the unfortunate, defends those who are innocent and helpless. And he describes himself as "more compassionate than cruel" (857).

Riquer tells us that this is the only point in the novel where the narrative becomes clearly historical. In 1611, after dominating the highways of Montseny, Segarra, and Barcelona, Rocaguinarda had accepted a pardon in exchange for service in Italy or Flanders, and had gone as captain of a regiment to Naples. Highway robbery was an endemic disease in Catalonia. The robber bands had friends and protectors in Barcelona, which explains why Roque commends Don Quixote to his Barcelonian friend Antonio Moreno. Furthermore, brigands were politically suspect because of their close connection with the French Huguenots. Apparently risking public censure, Cervantes gives us a somewhat favorable picture of Roque Guinart. In fact, Don Quixote becomes a mere spectator by comparison with the Catalonian robber (See RIQ, 159-162).

But although Rocaguinarda is a historical figure, by introducing him into a work of fiction and juxtaposing him with Don Quixote, Cervantes transcends the historical; the closest parallel to Roque Guinart is Don Quixote himself. But the Don's motivating ideals contrast rather than compare with those of Roque, who has chosen his career from a desire for revenge. As in other situations, Cervantes introduces characters who show the reader that, mad as his hero may be, he is less mad than those who claim to be sane. Don Quixote advises Roque Guinart to leave his calling; " 'I will teach you to be a knight-errant,' " he says (863). But Roque only laughs and changes the subject.

Cervantes' genius consists to a large extent in his brilliant handling of character. His plot itself, like the story of Claudia Jeronima in this chapter, is often commonplace. But into this plot Cervantes introduces a great many subsidiary figures who serve to reflect, like the surfaces of a prism, all the facets of the main character. And not only do they reflect Don Quixote, but

they are in one way or another distortions of him, so that they
form a commentary on him and vice-versa. Roque Guinart is
famous for his adventures as Don Quixote is for his knight-
errantry. But whereas Roque has under his control many groups
of bandits and a wide area of operation, Don Quixote has only
Sancho and not even the road on which he travels. Roque Guinart continues in his career despite his conscience; Don Quixote
continues in his *because of* his conscience. They represent two
different types of involvement in the affairs of men. Roque Guinart's robberies and restitutions succeed; Don Quixote's sallies
almost always fail. In fact, Don Quixote and Sancho are completely disregarded as Roque intercedes in the affair of Claudia
Jeronima. By and large Roque's decisions are fair ones, and
travelers are grateful to him for leaving them with at least part
of their money; Don Quixote's decisions often misfire and are
unintentionally biased. Roque's bandits, although they occasion-
ally grumble that he is more "like a friar than a highwayman"
(864), are loyal; if they are discontented, he threatens them with
his sword. Sancho, although loyal, dares to pin his master to the
ground. But when the two are placed side by side, most readers
would choose to follow the Don rather than Roque Guinart with
all his success in highway robbery. Mad as he is, Don Quixote inspires a basic trust because the reader sees that he becomes involved with others with the intention of healing wounds and
redressing wrongs whereas Roque Guinart is involved in his
calling in order to keep a personal feud open and festering. Don
Quixote is positively oriented toward others; if Roque Guinart
does assist others, it is as a by-product of a life based on selfish
gratification of his desire for revenge. "Compassionate and good-
natured" (862) as he may be, he has allowed the motive of vengeance to involve him, as he tells Don Quixote, "in the labyrinth
of confusions." (862) If anyone is also involved in a labyrinth of
confusions, it is, of course, Don Quixote himself. Thus Cervantes
skillfully deploys the characters so that whereas at one moment
they seem to foil one another and at the next to become parallel
figures, they always serve to comment on one another and to enlighten the whole subject of human behavior.

Chapter 61

An interesting aspect of this final section of the book is that for the first time Don Quixote encounters real violence, violence which is not a distortion of reality created by Don Quixote or by others (See RIQ, 163-167). Basilio's blood in the scene of Camacho's wedding had been a ruse. But now we meet a young woman, Claudia Jeronima, who has mortally wounded the lover who had deserted her. She may be compared with Dorothea, who had reacted quite differently to Don Ferdinand's desertion of her. Furthermore, Roque Guinart does not hesitate to split the head of a follower who criticizes him too loudly. Later, during the battle on the galley, two men fall dead beside Don Quixote. Such scenes, against which Don Quixote's own exploits seem pale, are one means whereby Cervantes prepares us for the demise of his hero. In the matter of Claudia Jeronima, Don Quixote has been ignored; and later, in the battle with the Turkish brig, Don Quixote is a mere onlooker. No one listens to him when he says (in Chapter 64) that he should be sent to rescue Don Gaspar Gregorio. These episodes are a fitting prelude not only to his defeat by the Knight of the White Moon, but to his own final recognition of the folly of his knighthood. In these episodes Cervantes gradually moves his hero away from stage center, thereby directing his sharp criticisms at the empty forms and bookish idealisms which have misled Don Quixote into a life of folly. One could hardly expect otherwise from one who had fought at Lepanto. But Cervantes is also a writer, one who creates the bookish idealisms he purports to criticize. In other words, neither those who split the heads of others for no real reason at all nor those who are engaged in pretending to split the heads of others for very *good* reasons are in the right. The violence in this final part of the novel, although it may make the activities of Don Quixote seem pale, at the same time reasserts the splendor of his motives of justice, of mercy, and of protection for the weak.

*   *   *

Leaving Roque Guinart after three days to his life of subter-fuge, Don Quixote and Sancho proceed to Barcelona. (Roque had been forced to hide himself from the world; the Duke and Duchess had hidden themselves only from Don Quixote and Sancho; Don Quixote and Sancho hide themselves from no one.) The day on which Don Quixote enters Barcelona is introduced with another mock heroic opening—"the fair face of dawn began to peep" (866)—for Don Quixote's exploits in Barcelona will be anything but heroic. For instance, neither Don Quixote nor Sancho has ever seen the sea before, and Sancho thinks the great ships must have feet in order to move; both are confounded by its size.

Don Quixote's welcome to the city is marred, however, by another fall—continuing the symbolism of descent already noted in the 1615 *Quixote*. Some boys tie furze to the tails of Rocinante and Dapple, and in a frenzy, the animals throw Don Quixote and Sancho to the ground. This is indeed a fitting overture to the Don's visit to Barcelona, for it is here that he will at last be un-horsed by the Knight of the White Moon.

Chapter 62

Don Quixote's host in Barcelona turns out to be another nobleman of the same stamp as the Duke. Don Antonio Moreno's first act is to display Don Quixote on a balcony in his doublet, to the great amusement of all passers-by; his second is to deceive Don Quixote about a supposedly enchanted head he owns; his third is to ride him through the streets with a sign proclaiming his name on his back, subjecting him to the taunts of the populace. One Castilian shouts that Don Quixote would have done less harm had he been "mad in private" (871), a point already made in these pages, for it is his attempts to implement his ideas which have so often been disastrous to himself and to others. And as the Castilian points out, Don Quixote's mission is contagious; others, like Don Antonio and his retinue, become infected by it. Cervantes creates this curious ambiguity about most people who come into contact with the Don. While, like the Duke and Duchess, they mock him and think him "highly amusing," they at the same time become involved in his madness, so that they often appear madder than he does.

Later a ball is held to afford "harmless amusement" to Don Antonio and his friends, but Don Quixote is so shaken by two would-be seductresses that he sits down in the middle of the dance floor and must be carried to bed. All of this underlines again frivolity and superficiality of most noblemen's lives by comparison with Don Quixote's. In fact, the point has been made so often that the reader wonders whether this episode, as well as the later reappearance of Altisidora, is really necessary. Furthermore, the questioning of the enchanted head seems to be a repetition, with slight variations, of the questioning of Master Peter's prophesying ape. Once more Don Quixote is thoroughly deceived. Just as the ape has symbolized his actor master, who is actually a criminal disguised as a puppeteer, so the enchanted head may be seen as a symbol of *its* owner, for it is informed by Don Antonio's nephew who speaks from a room below, just as those in power or authority often are informed by others behind the scenes.

The chapter closes with Don Quixote's visit to a printer's establishment where he makes the sage remark that translations are "like viewing Flemish tapestries from the wrong side" (877) and where he sees a copy of the imposter's continuation of the 1605 *Quixote*. Cervantes cannot resist a final thrust at this deceitful book, which he compares to the hog whose slaughter at Martinmas is inevitable.

Chapter 63

Let us follow Sancho alone for a moment. He has been disappointed by the words of the enchanted head which has told him he will govern now only in his own house. For although he says he has eschewed governing, the effects of the tortoise episode and of the fall into the pit have begun to fade, and he desires once more to rule and to be obeyed. Even a mock governorship has given him a taste for power. But during his visit to the galleys, he once more views hell, or what he judges to be hell. First, he is tossed from hand to hand by the crew, from starboard to larboard, reminiscent of the blanket tossing he received in the 1605 *Quixote;* as he stands panting and sweating a yard is lowered with a terrible noise, making him think the sky is falling in. He sees the oars by which the ships are propelled as red feet, and the flogging of the galley slaves convinces him that he is at least in purgatory. It is no wonder then that after Don Quixote's defeat by the Knight of the White Moon in Chapter 65, Sancho has again relinquished his ideas of governing, although stating wistfully that he has always wanted to be a count. His overriding attitude now is one of resignation. It is a long series of downfalls, of visits to hell, which bring both master and squire to their senses.

* * *

The adventure of the trip on the galley and the chase and capture of the pirate craft is the first time that war, a real war, has been made the subject of the narrative. The Turks were the most feared enemy of Christian Europe and had been fought by knights-errant in the chivalric romances thousands of times (RIQ, 166). Yet now, when Don Quixote has a *real* occasion to imitate Palmérin de Oliva, Esplandían, and all the others, he takes no part in the battle.

Still, the issue is not as simple as this. After the battle Anna Felix tells us that the brig was *not* approaching Barcelona for attack but for the purpose of putting her ashore. Thus the Spanish general has made the same sort of sally we have seen Don Quixote make again and again. He has attacked as an enemy one whose motives were innocent or even worthy and has endangered the life of an ally, Anna Felix. The general's action was, of course, necessary; what he does is motivated by duty, by an automatic military zeal. Don Quixote's actions, although not necessary, are motivated by both military and literary zeal (arms and letters). But the ideals of justice and mercy which Don Quixote brings to the practice of arms are seriously lacking in the general, who swears he will hang from the yard-arm every man he has captured. Even the Viceroy must later entreat him to desist from his plan. So although in a sense Don Quixote is eclipsed by the action of the battle scene, his absence in these pages serves to underline the fact that the values which accompanied his folly are now absent. Rather than ordering hanging from the yard-arm, Don Quixote would have demanded of his conquered foe a trip to El Toboso. True, a meaningless demand. But Cervantes seems to say in *Don Quixote*—better to have ideals and fail to realize them than not to have them at all. Don Quixote, as Maravall shows, believes in the perfectibility of man and the power of love to realize human ideals (MAR, 112). It is by comparison with these standards that the cruel hostility of Claudia Jeronima toward her 'lover,' of Roque Guinart toward a follower, and of the general toward his captives must be viewed.

*   *   *

The reunion of Anna Felix with her father, Ricote, is another episode which shows the results of the decrees to exile Moors from Spain in 1609 and 1613. Driven from their home, Ricote and his daughter have been judged worse than criminals. Sancho himself is still skeptical of Ricote's intentions; he avers that Anna Felix is Ricote's daughter but gives him no further credentials, although he says at the same time, "I know Ricote well" (886). It is only because Anna Felix and Ricote are Chris-

tians that they are helped by the assembled company at all; a
man's faith is a designation which may or may not attest to his
good character, yet only those Moors who turn Christians are
considered by Cervantes as worthy and acceptable people. Like
the story of the captive in the 1605 *Quixote,* the tale of the reunion of father and daughter and the rescue of Anna's lover is a
conventional one, complete with hairbreadth escapes and threats
to life and limb. What is of interest here is the strong feeling
against Moors—the result of chauvinism, religious fanaticism,
deep-rooted Moorish hostility to the state, and the threat they
represented of new invasions. Spanish control in Granada had
been established only within the past century, and conversion of
Moors to Christianity had been largely nominal. For these reasons, Cervantes and his characters always see Moors as outsiders,
inferiors, and enemies. But this example of a national animus
stands at such a distance in time that the modern reader is able
to see it in perspective and thereby to judge his own prejudices.
And although Cervantes makes it clear that he distrusts Moors,
at the same time he shows that there are certain Christian Moors
who have been unfairly discriminated against by Philip III's
decrees.

Chapters 64 and 65

The culminating adventure of the 1615 *Quixote* is the reappearance of Sampson Carrasco, this time as the Knight of the
White Moon. The white moon is a symbol of winter and death
in contrast to a yellow harvest moon; the moon also symbolizes
lunacy to which Quixote has fallen prey and which will at last
defeat him. As David Grossvogel points out, Carrasco's disguise
is meant to usurp Don Quixote's significance (GRO, 96). As
Knight of the White Moon, Carrasco assumes Don Quixote's
mood, his wanness, and his lunacy. (In fact, the mirrors on his
armor in the earlier encounter had been shaped like moons.) It

is this defeat by Carrasco which is eventually to return Don Quixote to his senses and to his home. We have come full circle to the conclusion of his major exploits. It is Sancho who perceives that this battle may have "knocked out" his master's madness, just as he recognizes that his own hopes are now scattered. And Riquer shows that Don Quixote's speech, as he lies on the ground at the mercy of his opponent's lance, is for the first time free of chivalric archaisms which until now he has used copiously. He has removed the mask of bookish language and speaks as a man of his era (RIQ, 168).

The curious thing about Sampson Carrasco is that he has taken his defeat by Don Quixote so seriously that he has prepared and waited for months to encounter him again. His desire to vanquish Don Quixote has become far more than the game he took it for at the beginning of this book. But like Roque Guinart, he has been basely motivated to assume a role. As he said after his defeat at Don Quixote's hands, "it will not be the desire to restore him to his senses that will drive me after him, but the desire for revenge" (561). As Knight of the Mirrors he had acted half in jest. He is now in dead earnest, and he meets his opponent two-thirds of the way down the field. Like many others we have met, Sampson Carrasco has been drawn into the vortex of Don Quixote's mad dream; deluded by the idea of being a defeated knight, he attacks, in a frenzy of self-justification, a feeble old man. Although he would like to believe that what he does is for Don Quixote's own good, it is difficult for the objective viewer to see that this violent method of returning Don Quixote to his home is necessary. As Sampson Carrasco, the Bachelor, he would have been ashamed to offer physical combat to an aging neighbor; only because he imagines that he is a knight is this method of revenge acceptable to him. One of the Duke's trick scenes in which Don Quixote could have been ordered by Dulcinea to return home would have been just as effective but less dramatic. It is, of course, the dynamic aspect of Don Quixote's fantasy which brings the book alive and involves the reader himself in knight-errantry.

Ironically, the Viceroy gives license for the fight, thinking it nothing but a joke, and Don Antonio believes that all Carrasco's efforts will be in vain. Neither reckons with the fierce intensity of Don Quixote or the Bachelor. Quixote's return home is ensured by the fact that he will not break a promise made in the name of chivalry, but the Bachelor's earnestness has been motivated by more selfish concerns than chivalry toward an opponent. Herein lies the difference between the two knights, and both prove the Viceroy and Don Antonio to be wrong.

* * *

Felled by a man half his age, Don Quixote has remained six days in bed when the renegade returns with Don Gregorio, Anna Felix's lover. The Viceroy and Don Antonio now attempt to get permission for Anna Felix and Ricote to remain in Spain, although Ricote still insists that Philip III's decree exiling the Moors was "an heroic resolve" (895) and that neither prayers, promises, nor bribes will move the officer who expelled them. According to Ricote, "the whole body of our race is contaminated and rotten" (895), strong feelings for one who wishes his own exile and that of his daughter to come to an end. His words illustrate again the only means by which a Moor could hope to be accepted in sixteenth- and seventeenth-century Spain—a total renunciation of his own heritage, people, and identity. This contrasts sharply with Don Quixote's quest in this book, a quest for his own identity, which he has mistaken for that of a knight. As the battle with Sampson Carrasco has begun to show him, to assume his true identity he must return to his village and once more become Alonso Quixada; Ricote, on the other hand, is forced by this same society to adopt an identity which is *not* his but that of a Spanish Christian. Ricote's experience, coming as it does on the heels of Don Quixote's renunciation of his knighthood, throws doubt upon the wisdom of a society which expects one man to assume a false identity and another to abandon one. One wonders if such a society is capable of judging what true identity is, or of seeing that knighthood is more than donning armor and mounting a nag called Rocinante.

Chapter 66

In deep depression, Don Quixote and Sancho leave Barcelona. Sancho blames their ill-fortune on Fate, which is drunken,
capricious, and blind. But Don Quixote, with new-found insight,
counters that "every man is architect of his own destiny" (896),
and blames himself for not having recognized that Rocinante was
no match for his opponent's horse. At least he has kept his word
to engage in battle. It is this insight that each man is responsible
for what he is and what he becomes that will enable Don Quixote
to achieve self-knowledge at the end. His recognition of this
principle is one of the high points of his career, following, as it
does, his downfall at the hands of the Knight of the White Moon.
It even implies his rejection of such agents as enchanters. As Don
Quixote begins to see, "the ultimate reality of the world is neither
matter nor spirit, is no definite thing, but a perspective" (ORT,
45). It is not knight-errantry, but what he makes of knight-
errantry that is important. Quite by chance Sampson Carrasco
has accomplished far more than he intended in his quest for
revenge.

It is, therefore, doubly tragic to see Don Quixote at the end
of the chapter still insist that Tosilos is enchanted. The lackey
tells them that he has been given a hundred strokes for disobey-
ing the Duke, that his girl has become a nun, and that Doña
Rodriguez has returned to Castile. As in the matter of Andrew in
the 1605 *Quixote,* as soon as the knight has turned his back all
hell breaks loose, and any good work he may have accidentally
achieved has quickly been undone by the callousness of others.
Despite Don Quixote's earlier insight that "every man is architect
of his own destiny," his failure, reflected in Tosilos' story, is too
much for him to face honestly, and he takes refuge in the fantasy
that enchanters have been at work. Instead of accepting defeat,
he substitutes a fiction to enable him to disguise it. It is only
when he will be able to see that Tosilos *is* the lackey whom he

met in the lists and that his own actions in the encounter have been futile that Don Quixote will begin to understand his own maxim that true knighthood is knighthood of the spirit. Cervantes refuses to give the reader even the small satisfaction of seeing Don Quixote, in his delusion, unite a lackey and a servant girl.

Although Don Quixote is by his own admission "shaken and shattered," Sancho in this chapter judges his last case with the same acumen and wisdom he had displayed in his governorship. Don Quixote is moving fitfully toward self-awareness, but Sancho seems already to have achieved a good measure of it.

Chapter 67

In any episode Cervantes' meanings are likely to be multiple. It is this ambiguity which gives his book its depth. Thus although the Gentlemen in Green is exemplary in many ways, he also has his flaws, and although the Duke and Duchess are on the whole careless and frivolous, they have some generous feelings. Cervantes seems to acquiesce in the Spanish attitude toward Moors, yet at the same time he may satirize it through Sancho, who calls Ricote an enemy in one sentence and a friend in the next, or indirectly through Ricote himself, who in attempting to become a Spaniard states that his whole race is contaminated. Cervantes deals likewise with the literary traditions of the day. Satire of books of chivalry appears everywhere, of course, but the chivalric ideal is never derided. Like Don Quixote, Gines de Pasamonte may be seen as a take-off on the conventional rogue figure. Roque Guinart, although in some ways authentic as a rogue, is less authentic when we consider his motives for becoming one. Even the romance may be parodied in the overblown plots of love and intrigue involving such 'model' heroines as Anna Felix, Claudia Jeronima, or Doña Rodriguez' daughter.

It is equally difficult to settle on one interpretation of the pastoral scenes. Does Cervantes side with Marcela, or is there an element of irony in her story? Is the golden age represented by the goatherds as golden as it seems to Don Quixote? And is the netting of little birds by the shepherds and shepherdesses on the road to Barcelona an act of cruelty or merely healthy amusement?

The conversation describing the intention of Don Quixote and Sancho to become shepherds is, however, full of obvious satire of the pastoral tradition, which offers even less a refuge for Don Quixote than the chivalric mode. Don Quixote sees it as a means of retreat for a year, during which he and Sancho will be equals rather than master and squire, one mourning absent beauty, the other celebrating constant love (presumably of Teresa). The literary source of Don Quixote's fantasies is clear in these passages, for, as Riquer shows, Don Quixote will imitate not *real* shepherds, but those found in pastoral romances of which, as we have seen from the inquisition of his library, he had read great numbers (RIQ, 169).

It would appear that Cervantes' attitude toward tradition of any kind becomes more and more ironic as his book progresses. The pastoral and romance traditions which had been treated more seriously in the 1605 *Quixote* are now the subject of obvious parody.

Chapter 68

In this chapter Don Quixote reaches one of the lowest points in his career: his trampling by a herd of hogs. This represents an even greater degradation than his previous trampling by bulls, for whereas the former episode had led to deep discouragement on the part of the knight, Don Quixote is now resigned to his punishment and sees it as "Heaven's just chastisement" (907), a proper sequel to his defeat by the Knight of the White Moon. It is possible to see now why this defeat has been therapeutic for Don Quixote and why it is the spiritual axis of the 1615 book. In accepting the reality of being vanquished, Don Quixote has gone a long way toward recognizing who he is, an aging man on a feeble nag, a man whose judgment may seriously err. Once this point has been established in his mind, he is able to talk about his "sin," presumably the sin of misinterpreting reality, both his own and that of Rocinante. Although the trampling by the hogs may seem superfluous in the light of all the previous tramplings, Don Quixote's reaction to it is different; he shows a new recognition of his suffering as self-induced, which is a necessary step in achieving a return to sanity.

Chapters 69 and 70

The return of Don Quixote and Sancho to the Duke's castle and the silly ruses which accompany the death of Altisidora are an appropriate sequel to the trampling by the hogs. Once more the pair is dishonored as six waiting women slap and pinch Sancho. But Don Quixote is not quite sure that Altisidora has really died, and Sancho rebels when the waiting women start to prick him with pins. As in the episode of the hogs, both have gained a certain amount of insight since their previous stay at the castle, and Sancho sees that there are enchantments in the world from which he cannot deliver himself (914), suggesting that he now recognizes the reality of true power, as opposed to his own puppeteering as "governor." He will always, to some extent, be at its mercy. And yet Cervantes finally states in no uncertain terms what we have pointed out many times above: Cide Hamete, he tells us, "considers the mockers as mad as their victims" (916). The Duke and Duchess are fools to play such tricks, Altisidora the pawn of madmen. Don Quixote's advice as he leaves the castle, that Altisidora should be kept occupied with needlework, is the sanest remark that has been made in the entire episode. In fact, the Duke and Duchess and their whole retinue suffer from idleness which Cervantes shows to be at the root of all their frivolous entertainments. As usual, Don Quixote has the last word in his encounters with other characters, defeated and dishonored though he may be.

* * *

In the scene in Don Quixote's bedroom, Sancho does not bother to ask Altisidora about Heaven, for it is a foregone conclusion with him that she has been in Hell. As Don Quixote shrinks down into his bed, retreating before Altisidora's charms, she discloses a scene she witnessed at the gates of Hell—a dozen devils playing tennis with books stuffed with wind and fluff. As they play, the books are knocked to pieces and scattered. Once more Cervantes enjoys a satiric thrust at other authors—first, at critics, who are like the devils playing ball while destroying the means by which they play, and second, at the imposter from Tordesillas whose sequel to the 1605 *Quixote* is presumably among those books destroyed by the devils, a thing full of wind and fluff.

Chapter 71

Sancho has been extremely dilatory about starting on his whippings in the disenchantment of Dulcinea. Don Quixote has even waked him in the middle of the night to beg him to begin his flagellations, but Sancho has insisted: "I can't persuade myself that the flogging of my posterior has anything to do with the disenchanting of the enchanted" (901), and Don Quixote's suggestions of timely moments to start (such as during their confinement among the galley slaves or after the slappings by the six waiting women) seem to Sancho especially untimely. Only after Don Quixote offers to pay him and later to double his pay does Sancho agree to his task, but chooses to lash himself among a grove of trees, stripping them of bark instead of himself of skin.

Altisidora has reneged on her promise to give Sancho her smocks in return for his restoring her to life, and Sancho has made much of the fact that he has received nothing from his governorship. "I entered naked, and naked I am now" (828) has been repeated many times. Despite the fact that Sancho is naked among his grove of trees, he intends to make sure that this time he will not emerge from the experience still naked. We see that Sancho has clearly gained in his ability to assess a situation and the motives of others in imposing tasks upon him.

At the same time, as we have seen in the episode of the hogs and in the revival of Altisidora, Don Quixote has gained in self-knowledge. As he and Sancho arrive at the next inn, he views it as an inn and not as a castle, for Cervantes tells us that "since his defeat he spoke on all subjects with a sounder judgment" (924). It will be remembered that Don Quixote's defeats in the 1605 *Quixote* were usually followed by new outbreaks of madness. It is clear that Cervantes has intended the encounter with the Knight of the White Moon to be a turning point in Don Quixote's development—a traumatic experience which provides him with new insight. It is here that Don Quixote begins his return to sanity despite the vengeful motives of Sampson Carrasco. The episodes which follow this battle show the evolution of Don Quixote's growing self-knowledge. As Sancho says on once more viewing their village at the end of the next chapter, "Don Quixote, . . . though conquered by another, has conquered himself" (930). What Sancho has gained in knowledge of others in the failure of his governorship, Don Quixote has gained in self-knowledge by his defeat at the hands of the Knight of the White Moon.

Chapter 72

It is in this chapter that Cervantes at last disposes of the imposter who has written the continuation of the 1605 *Quixote*, a man who has haunted him throughout the pages of this volume. On meeting Don Alvaro Tarfe, a character who appears in the imposter's work, Don Quixote and Sancho are able quickly to discredit him, and they persuade him to sign an affidavit declaring that it is not Don Quixote who is the subject of the imposter's book. It is noteworthy that here the Don resorts to legal methods rather than to arms. Earlier he would doubtless have challenged Don Alvaro in the lists. Don Quixote's new-found prudence reminds one this time of the Gentleman in Green.

Chapter 73

As Don Quixote and Sancho re-enter their native village, for the first time in his career as knight, Don Quixote is disturbed by two omens. As with most passages in Cervantes' work, a dual interpretation of these lines on omens is possible. To begin with, they are mock heroic passages, parodies of the verses on soothsaying and interpretation of omens found in the *Odyssey*, the *Iliad*, or Greek drama. As such they set a satiric tone for Don Quixote's return as a defeated hero. At the same time, they reflect Don Quixote's inner state at this point and thereby set a tone of pathos. Inwardly Don Quixote knows that his quest is finished and that he will never again view Dulcinea, although on a conscious level he has been saying that his retreat from knight-errantry is for a year only. Whereas the omens themselves are shown to be empty of meaning (Sancho at once transforms both

incidents into signs of good fortune), Don Quixote's interpretations are significant symbolically, showing the reader that indeed
both he and Sancho "will never see it [knighthood] again" (931).
In Cervantes' writing, it is this combination of wit and pathos
that saves the pathos from becoming maudlin and the wit from
becoming frivolous.

*   *   *

The re-entry of Don Quixote into his village may be compared with the two previous returns. After his first short sally
in the 1605 *Quixote* he had come back wounded, mounted on an
ass, and accompanied by the laborer from the village. At the end
of the 1605 book he returned lying on a pile of hay in an ox
wagon, wounded in mind and in body, and accompanied by the
priest, the barber, and Sancho. (It may be remembered that
Lancelot was forced to ride in a cart when he left to rescue
Queen Guinevere. Don Quixote is not leaving on a mission, but
returning from an unsuccessful one.)

Now, however, at the end of the 1615 book, Don Quixote
returns unwounded, mounted on Rocinante, and accompanied by
Sancho, as he had departed in Chapter 7. Despite the insights that
he has gained, the re-entry is a mock-triumphal one, attended by
a crowd of gaping boys and by Dapple, adorned with a mitre (one
of Sancho's jokes). The previous re-entries have been involuntary
ones made necessary by Don Quixote's physical and mental condition. Now, however, in accordance with the rules of chivalry,
Don Quixote has chosen to return as a vanquished knight-errant.
Had he chosen to discount his defeat at the hands of the Knight
of the White Moon or to become Alonso Quixano the Good in
Barcelona, Cervantes' parody would have remained unfinished. It
is fitting that the knight-errantry which has inspired Don Quixote's career should also motivate his final return to his village in
the manner of knights of old. It is total proof of his loyalty to
his ideal. At the same time, as the mock omens in this chapter
suggest, Don Quixote knows that Dulcinea (the fiction of chivalry)
will not reappear. For as Mia Gerhardt shows, it is Don Quixote
who has created Dulcinea as he has created himself. And since he

is not a poet and lacks the ability to execute his ideas, Dulcinea is from the beginning an indefinite figure (GER, 40-46).

Here Cervantes' double meaning is evident. Not only has Don Quixote's madness been cured, but the purpose for which the book has been written, the end of *all* books of chivalry, has been attained. "I shall never see Dulcinea again" (930) truly prophesies the end of the chivalric mode of which *Don Quixote* is the last example. That Cervantes can say this with some certainty indicates the hope and confidence with which he issues this work. For according to Cide Hamete, without a doubt absurd stories of knight-errantry "will soon tumble to the ground" (940). The pervasive influence of *Don Quixote* had been foreseen as early as Chapter 3, when Sampson Carrasco had told the Don: "there cannot be any nation into whose tongue it will not be translated" (486).

* * *

Before Don Quixote's demise, Cervantes disposes of his hero's pastoral dream. The pastoral existence involves no active quest as does knight-errantry. No maidens are to be rescued, no afflicted persons saved. The shepherd's existence is a passive one—which in literary tradition is largely idle and artificial. For Don Quixote it is more in the nature of a retreat, a retreat that has been forced upon him by his downfall at Sampson's hands. (A different stress is given to Christ's shepherding of His flocks, the emphasis here lying on the active saving of souls.) Sampson Carrasco and the priest both agree to join Don Quixote as shepherds (in the same way as they have already played roles in his chivalric fantasy), both hoping that Don Quixote will at least be cured of his knightly delusions and neither recognizing that his new fantasy may be more deadly than his first.

One fantasy may replace the other, but it is clear from an analysis of the two that the pastoral dream is far less noble in intent and that a novel about the shepherd Quixotiz would quickly pall. Niece and housekeeper both object to Don Quixote's latest scheme. Curiously, their words echo those of the Gentleman in Green: to "stay at home, look after your property, confess frequently, be good to the poor" (934. Cf. 567).

Chapter 74

Having taken to his bed, Don Quixote falls prey to a fever and during his illness finds his judgment restored. Abruptly he rejects the folly of profane histories of chivalry and recognizes his identity as that of Alonso Quixano, the Good. "I was mad, but I am sane now," he announces. (938) He even makes the provision, in leaving his estate to his niece, that she marry a man who does not know what books of chivalry are.

Although it is academic to ask exactly what kind of existence Alonso Quixano would have pursued had he lived, the manner of his death is clear. He wishes to renounce his addiction to chivalric tales but in so doing he says "my death shall turn them to my profit" (936). Cervantes seems to hint here that his hero, aware of the legend he has created (for he knows that he already is the subject of at least two books), now hopes that others reading of his quest for the good, the beautiful, and the true may see his high-minded intentions and where he has failed. They may thereby avoid his pitfalls in carrying on the mission he has begun. It is in this hope that Don Quixote dies in "so calm and Christian a manner" (939). His apotheosis is accomplished, in fact, by Cide Hamete Benengeli who writes, "For me alone Don Quixote was born and I for him. His was the power of action, mine of writing. Only we two are at one. . . ." (940) (Banish all thoughts of the man from Tordesillas.) Mia Gerhardt shows that the tension which charges the entire book is thus abolished, for Cide, who represents "la vie écrite" (the written life), and Don Quixote, who represents "la vie vécue" (the lived life), are thus harmoniously fused. What Don Quixote dreams is what Cide affirms. Reality and illusion serve rather than oppose one another (GER, 56).

But it is necessary to turn for a moment to Sancho. At Don Quixote's death he becomes a tragic figure, for he can no longer travel the roads as a knight's squire, and having experienced the high excitement of the chivalric dream, he will be unable to return to his farm, to Teresa and his cabbages. Raymond Willis shows that he is thus a prototype of the modern fictional hero, "a stranger to himself and an exile in his own land" (WS, 227).

Don Quixote has emerged from the depths of his own defeats with a new sense of his identity. No man's ideals can be fulfilled in a lifetime and by him alone. Don Quixote, like all men who have pursued dreams, had mounted his Rocinante and set forth to do battle against insuperable odds. In his parting words Cervantes tells us that his object has been to arouse contempt for tales of chivalry—which is indeed the warning of Don Quixote's entire existence; if we are to carry on for him, we must heed his failure in the practice of arms and avoid assuming a false identity in pursuing a worthy goal. The full meaning of the various discussions on arms and letters now comes into focus. Cervantes shows us that the wise man integrates his ideals and his methods of achieving them, combining the best of Sancho Panza and of Don Quixote; the writing of the story of Don Quixote, is, in fact, such an integration of means and ends. For Cervantes' book proposes, as Don Quixote himself had proposed to the Gentleman in Green, that a true knight, versed in the practice of arms, will be: "chaste in his thoughts, straightforward in his words, liberal in his works, valiant in his deeds, patient in his afflictions, charitable towards the needy, and, in fact, a maintainer of truth [whatever that may be, we hear Cervantes cavil], although its defence may cost him his life" (583).

Bibliography and Key

AU   Auden, W. H. *The Dyer's Hand*. New York: Random House, 1962.

CAS   Casalduero, Joaquin. *Sentido y forma del Quijote*. Madrid: Ediciones Insula, 1949. See also "The Composition of 'Don Quixote' " in *Cervantes Across the Centuries*, ed. Angel Flores and M. J. Benardete. New York: Dryden Press, 1947.

OB   Cervantes, Miguel de. *Obras completas*, ed. Martín de Riquer. Barcelona: Editorial Planeta, 1962, Vol. 1.

COL   *Cervantes. A Collection of Critical Essays*, ed. Lowry Nelson. Englewood Cliffs, N.J.: Prentice-Hall, Inc., 1969.

CUR   Curtius, Ernst. *European Literature and the Latin Middle Ages*, trans. Willard R. Trask. New York: Pantheon Books, 1952.

GER   Gerhardt, Mia. *Don Quijote, la vie et les livres*. Amsterdam: Noord-Hollandsche Uitg. Mij., 1955.

GRO   Grossvogel, David I. "Cervantes: *Don Quixote*" in *Limits of the Novel*. Ithaca, New York: Cornell University Press, 1968.

IM   Immerwahr, Raymond. "Structural Symmetry in the Episodic Narratives of *Don Quijote*, Part One." *Comparative Literature*, 10 (1958), 121-135.

K   Kaiser, Walter. "The Last Fool" in *Praisers of Folly*. Cambridge, Massachusetts: Harvard University Press, 1963.

MAR   Maravall, José Antonio. *El Humanismo de las armas en 'Don Quijote.'* Madrid: Instituto de Estudios Politicos, 1948.

ME   Meyer, Herman. *The Poetics of Quotation in the European Novel,* trans. Theodore and Yetta Ziolkowski. Princeton, New Jersey: Princeton University Press, 1968.

NEL   Nelson, Jr., Lowry. *Baroque Lyric Poetry.* New Haven, Conn.: Yale University Press, 1961.

ORT   Ortega y Gasset, José. *Meditations on Quixote,* trans. Evelyn Rugg and Diego Marin. New York: W. W. Norton and Co., 1961.

PF   Parker, Alexander A. "Fielding and the Structure of *Don Quixote.*" *Bulletin of Hispanic Studies,* 33 (1956), 1-16.

PL   ———. *Literature and the Delinquent.* Edinburgh: Edinburgh University Press, 1967.

PRE   Predmore, R. L. *The World of Don Quixote.* Cambridge, Massachusetts: Harvard University Press, 1967.

RI   Riley, E. C. *Cervantes' Theory of the Novel.* Oxford: Clarendon Press, 1962.

RIQ   Riquer, Martín de. *Aproximación al Quijote.* 2nd ed. Barcelona: Editorial Teide, S. A., 1967.

RUS   Russell, P. E. *"Don Quijote* as a Funny Book." *Modern Language Review,* 64 (1969), 302-326.

SAR   Sarmiento, Edward. "On the Interpretation of *Don Quixote.*" *Bulletin of Hispanic Studies,* 37 (1960), 146-153.

SP   Spitzer, Leo. "Linguistic Perspectivism in the *Don Quijote*" in *Linguistics and Literary History,* Princeton, N.J.: Princeton University Press, 1948.

T   Togeby, Knud. *La Composition du roman "Don Quijote."* Supp. 1 of *Orbis Litterarum.* Copenhagen: 1957.

UN   Unamuno, Miguel de. *Our Lord Don Quixote,* trans. Anthony Kerrigan. *Selected Works of Miguel de Unamuno,* Vol. 3. Princeton, N.J.: Princeton University Press, 1967.

VAN   Van Doren, Mark. *Don Quixote's Profession.* New York: Columbia University Press, 1958.

WARD   Wardropper, Bruce W. *"Don Quixote:* Story or History?" *Modern Philology* 63 (1965), 1-11.

WP   Willis, Jr., Raymond S. *The Phantom Chapters of the Quijote.* New York: Hispanic Institute of the United States, 1953.

WS   ———. "Sancho Panza: Prototype for the Modern Novel." *Hispanic Review,* 37 (1969), 207-227.

(Page numbers without prefixes all refer to the Penguin Classics edition of *Don Quixote* translated by J. M. Cohen.)

Index